DATA
BABY

DATA BABY

MY LIFE IN A PSYCHOLOGICAL EXPERIMENT

SUSANNAH BRESLIN

LEGACY
LIT

New York Boston

Legacy Lit
Hachette Book Group
1290 Avenue of the Americas
New York, NY 10104
LegacyLitBooks.com
Twitter.com/LegacyLitBooks
Instagram.com/LegacyLitBooks

First Edition: November 2023

Legacy Lit is an imprint of Grand Central Publishing. The Legacy Lit name and logo are trademarks of Hachette Book Group, Inc.

The Hachette Speakers Bureau provides a wide range of authors for speaking events. To find out more, go to hachettespeakersbureau.com or email HachetteSpeakers@hbgusa.com.

The publisher is not responsible for websites (or their content) that are not owned by the publisher.

Legacy Lit books may be purchased in bulk for business, educational, or promotional use. For information, please contact your local bookseller or the Hachette Book Group Special Markets Department at special.markets@hbgusa.com.

Print book interior design by Marie Mundaca.

Library of Congress Cataloging-in-Publication Data
Names: Breslin, Susannah, author.
Title: Data baby : my life in a psychological experiment / Susannah Breslin.
Description: New York : Legacy Lit, 2023.
Identifiers: LCCN 2023026353 | ISBN 9780306926006 (hardcover) |
    ISBN 9780306925993 (ebook)
Subjects: LCSH: Breslin, Susannah. | Breslin, Susannah—Psychology. |
    Harold E. Jones Child Study Center. | Personality development—
    Research—United States. | Child psychology—Research—United
    States. | Human experimentation in psychology—Moral and ethical
    aspects—United States. | Breast—Cancer—Patients—United States—
    Biography. | Women journalists—United States—Biography.
Classification: LCC BF723.P4 B74 2023 | DDC 155.2/5—dc23/
    eng/20230707
LC record available at https://lccn.loc.gov/2023026353

ISBNs: 9780306926006 (hardcover), 9780306925993 (ebook)

Printed in the United States of America

LSC-C

Printing 1, 2023

for girls
with stories to tell
and secrets to keep

We accept the reality of the world with
which we're presented.
It's as simple as that.

—*The Truman Show*

AUTHOR'S NOTE

This is the story of my quest to understand how a psychological experiment that studied my life and the lives of over a hundred other Berkeley children for three decades and predicted who we would grow up to be shaped my life and the person I became.

With the exception of my own, the names, some identifying details, and the individual case numbers of the subjects who were studied in the experiment have been changed.

This book reflects my present recollections of experiences over time. Some events have been compressed, and some dialogue has been re-created.

DATA
BABY

ONE

As I understood it, my life in a psychological experiment began on the day I was born. At 1:38 a.m., on April 10, 1968, I was delivered in the maternity ward of an Oakland, California, hospital. According to my mother, I was a hideous baby. Instead of having two distinct eyebrows, my eyebrows met in the middle to form one long horizontal brow, otherwise known as a mono-brow, which, while flattering on the Mexican painter Frida Kahlo or the basketball player Anthony Davis, was unsettling on a newborn. Due to a severe case of jaundice, my skin and the whites of my eyes were a curious shade of yellow, giving me a radioactive glow. And my skull was grossly misshapen, the result of the compression my cranium had undergone as I journeyed down my mother's vaginal canal. Unsure what to do (as if there was anything to be done) or say (as if there was anything to say) about my unfortunate countenance, the obstetrician cut the umbilical cord and thrust me in the direction of my mother.

At the time, my father—handsome, athletic, thirty-three, six-foot-four, from Brooklyn, New York—was a poetry professor at the University of California, Berkeley, and my mother—attractive (in a nerdy sort of way), svelte (when not pregnant), thirty (coincidentally, I had arrived on her birthday), five-foot-eleven, from Allentown, Pennsylvania—was an English instructor at UC Extension. They had met while pursuing their respective doctorates at the University of Minnesota and had relocated to the San Francisco Bay Area after my father had secured a tenure-track faculty position in the English department at UC Berkeley. While they intended to start a family eventually, my sister, who was born three and a half years earlier, had been an accident. I had been planned.

In those days, doctors believed that if a husband (say, my father) were to witness his wife (say, my mother) laboring to eject a small human being (say, me) from her vagina as she sprawled on a delivery table awash in a mess of her sweat, urine, and fecal matter, it could ruin a couple's sex life. As a result, my father had been banished to a waiting room down the hall (such rooms were known as Stork Clubs), where he had spent the last several hours pacing, smoking, and eyeing the wall clock, alongside the other stressed-out, impatient, flustered fathers-to-be. Finally, the waiting room door opened, the nurse called my father's name, and he was informed that both mother and child were resting comfortably and could be seen shortly. One of the other men offered him a cigar. Another man clapped him on the back. *Thank god*, my father, who was an atheist, thought.

"She'll be tall," he observed some time later, standing sentinel next to a hospital bed occupied by my mother. A nurse had propped her up with pillows and tucked me into the nook of her arm. He was relieved that I was healthy, that I had all of my fingers and toes, and that I was mostly shaped like a normal baby, but he had been hoping for a boy. He had wanted a son to teach how to play basketball. Given my height, which he projected would be exceptional, *I* could be taught to play basketball, he hypothesized. He started planning how to teach me layups.

My mother, whose long wavy red hair was tied loosely back and who was wearing a white hospital gown with a cornflower pattern, didn't respond. As a post-delivery flood of oxytocin and endorphins coursed through her system, she scrutinized my visage, seeking to divine my future. Trying to ignore my unpleasant eyebrows (*eyebrow?* she corrected herself), yellowish hue, and oddly shaped head, she surveyed my large forehead, long eyelashes, and round face that reminded her of Richard M. Nixon, who was then campaigning to be the next president of the United States. It was hard to tell at this stage. Perhaps I would be a teacher, or a writer, or some other thing having to do with language, or words, or books (like my parents), she speculated hopefully.

"Have you got it?"

My father nodded and patted the pocket of his green army coat, which he had bought at a secondhand store. It had previously belonged to a soldier who had fought in a war that my father had no interest in fighting and into which he was exempted from being drafted.

"I should get going. I don't want to be late." He patted my mother's left leg, which was sticking out from underneath the sheet, presuming that would suffice. "Will you be all right while I'm gone? I shouldn't be longer than an hour."

"We'll be here."

He brushed my mother's cheek with a perfunctory kiss.

In the parking lot, he slid behind the steering wheel of a beige four-door 1967 Dodge Dart. He started the engine and drove out of the lot, heading north. He crossed the city border and entered Berkeley. Two blocks south of the university, he parked on the west side of a predominantly residential street. In the distance, he could see, the Berkeley Hills were shrouded in fog, the white tendrils curling around the tops of the redwood, pine, and eucalyptus trees.

He was early, so he settled in to wait. His light-brown hair was thinning at the top. He had circles under his green eyes, due to genetics and his propensity for worrying. Under his jacket, he wore a long-sleeved denim shirt; my mother had sewn a name patch over the left breast pocket that read JIM in red cursive and made him look more like a gas station attendant than a college professor, which was how he preferred it. My mother had sewn purple-and-gold ribbon to the bottom hem of his bell-bottom jeans, elongating them to accommodate his long legs. On his size 14, extra-wide feet he wore a pair of brown leather lace-up ankle boots with white rubber soles.

From the driver's seat my father eyed the low-lying complex across the street, which consumed most of the block. It comprised two single-story, flat-roofed, warm-orange stucco structures with dark redwood piping that had been rendered in the Bay Area modernist style. The rectangular building to the north held the administrative offices; the T-shaped building to the south contained the classrooms. On the right-hand side, a tall, dark redwood fence extended to the corner and obscured the outdoor play yards from view by any curious passersby. In front, a natural wood sign with white painted letters planted in a bed of ivy and framed by purple plum trees read:

UNIVERSITY OF CALIFORNIA

HAROLD E. JONES
CHILD STUDY CENTER
2425 ATHERTON STREET

Four decades earlier, a pioneering initiative led by the Laura Spelman Rockefeller Memorial had funded the establishment of child studies institutes at half a dozen universities across North America: Yale University, Columbia University, the University of Iowa, the University of Minnesota, the University of Toronto, and UC Berkeley, the only Rockefeller-funded research institute in the West. At UC Berkeley, the Institute of Child Welfare planned to "study the factors that affect human development from the earliest stages of life." But its researchers had needed children to study. An exclusive laboratory preschool had offered a win-win solution: The university's faculty and staff got convenient, affordable, quality child-care and its researchers and students got young human subjects.

Originally, the preschool had been housed in a large, rambling wood house on the south side of campus, where a screened pavilion allowed researchers to observe the children while they played in the yard. From the beginning, it had been of the utmost importance that the children *not* know that they were being studied; if the children had realized someone was watching them, they might have changed their behavior, due to "the observer effect," the phenomenon by which the act of observing something changes that which is being observed.

By the late 1950s, the Institute of Child Welfare had been renamed the Institute of Human Development, and the preschool's ad hoc home had fallen into disrepair and been condemned. The university had enlisted Joseph Esherick, a tall, laconic UC Berkeley architecture professor, to design a new building. Esherick—who went on to design The Cannery, a shopping center in San Francisco, the demonstration houses at Sea Ranch up the coast in Sonoma County, and the Monterey Bay Aquarium down the coast in Monterey; who, in 1989, was awarded a gold medal by the American Institute of Architects, putting him in the company of Frank Lloyd Wright, Le Corbusier, and I. M. Pei; and who liked to say, "The ideal kind of building is one you don't see"—had never designed a preschool before, much less one made for spying on children. In 1960, the Harold E. Jones Child Study Center, which had been named for the Institute of Human Development's late director, had opened its doors to great fanfare.

My father checked his watch. It was almost eight o'clock. Moving determinedly, he pushed open the driver's-side door, stepped out of the vehicle, and strode purposefully across the street. From the sidewalk, he made his way up the zigzagging entrance ramp. At the top of the ramp, he turned right, tracking east between the buildings along a concrete walkway under a dark redwood trellis canopied with translucent plastic panels in bright colors—ruby, tangerine, lemon, and turquoise—which on sunny days cast Technicolor shadows across the walls, windows, and walkways below. Three-quarters of the way down the path, he turned left. Moments later, he walked into the main office.

"Hello," a woman said from behind the front desk.

"Good morning." My father reached into his jacket pocket, from which he produced an envelope that contained an application for my enrollment. He handed it to her. "This is an application for my daughter."

She took the envelope.

"She's six and a half hours old," he said.

"Congratulations," she said, seemingly unsurprised.

"This is what we were told to do. Because of the waiting list."

"We appreciate your interest," she said and smiled enigmatically.

As my father retraced his steps, he picked up his pace. He had taken the day off from work, and now he had completed his mission. Tomorrow, he would drive to campus, where he had an office on the fourth floor of Wheeler Hall, a gray stone Classical Revival building. From the balcony, he would admire the view of Berkeley, the Bay, and the Golden Gate Bridge. Then he would go inside, sit down at his typewriter, and get back to writing his book.

———

Four years later, on an otherwise unremarkable mid-August morning in 1972, my mother stood on the cracked pavement of the driveway of the pale-pink stucco two-story house in which we lived near the bottom of a steep single-block street in a lower tier of the North Berkeley Hills. Her hair was short and curly, and she was wearing octagon-shaped glasses, a sleeveless bright-orange mini-dress, and brown leather sandals of the sort that might have been worn by Athena, the goddess of war and wisdom. She rolled her eyes and sighed loudly, yanking open the Dart's rear passenger-side door.

"For god's sake, stop *dawdling*!"

My mother's sharp tone snapped me out of my daydream as I loitered at the front porch's top stair. With a soft *pop!* my right thumb, which my mother had reminded me countless times to stop sucking ("You'll get buck teeth from that!"), fell from my mouth. I started down the stairs. In the backyard the day before, my mother had used her sewing shears to trim my light-brown hair into a short bob with bangs while my sister had galloped back and forth across the lawn on a broom that she was pretending was a horse, her favorite animal. For my first day of preschool, my mother had dressed me in a purple-and-pink paisley top and matching bell-bottom pants and white Keds sneakers.

"We're going to be *late!*"

Slowly, I walked down the front steps to the sidewalk and to the driveway. When I reached the car, I stared up at her. She stared down at me.

"Will you get *in!*" she cried. She pushed me into the back seat, buckled my seat belt, and slammed the door.

The letter from the Child Study Center had arrived in the mail that spring. In the foyer, the envelope in her hand, she had sent up a silent prayer (to a god in which she no longer believed but to which she reached out from time to time when she felt desperate enough) that I had been chosen. She tore it open. *We are delighted to accept Susannah for admission this fall,* the letter read. (Unfortunately, they had heard about the Child Study Center too late to enroll my sister, although she would attend a summer session that same year.) In the empty house, my mother shrieked with delight and then clamped her hand over her mouth to stifle her glee even though no one could have heard her.

The older of two daughters of two educators, she had graduated at the top of her class from Mount Holyoke College in South Hadley, Massachusetts. It is one of the Seven Sisters, the consortium of historically all-women colleges that were equivalent to the male-dominated Ivy League. The college's motto is Psalm 144:12: "That our daughters may be as corner stones, polished after the similitude of a palace." In Minneapolis, she had been working on her doctorate and had planned to pursue a career as an English professor when she met my father. He had been dating the department secretary, a comely woman with thick brunette hair and an hourglass figure, who had a young son (despite not being married, my mother had noted, scornfully), and had not been as smart as my mother was (my mother had deduced, feeling superior). My mother was thrilled to steal this good-looking, smart, clever guy away from a more conventionally attractive woman.

Instead of getting her PhD, my mother had gotten married. She followed my father to Berkeley, and then she got pregnant. She resigned herself to teaching part-time, and as her career floundered, my father's flourished. He was awarded his doctorate. He secured tenure. He published his first book, a survey of the works of the poet William Carlos Williams, which was well received.

As she backed out of the driveway, my mother thought about what she would do now that I was enrolled in the preschool and my sister was enrolled in a public grade school. She would complete her doctorate. She would become a professor, like my father. She would write a book of her own.

Ten minutes later, she was piloting the car around the Marin Circle, in the middle of which a concrete fountain decorated with bears balanced on their hind legs was belching a weak stream of water into the air, when she had a sudden realization: *I don't want to be a mother anymore.* She turned onto Los Angeles Avenue, feeling embarrassed and ashamed. But the truth of the matter was that motherhood was a never-ending, 24/7 *slog*, an unpaid job with no time off, a role that demanded she

occupy her time and her mind with meeting the cease-
less, frequently irrational demands of two people who
were far smaller and significantly less well educated than
she was. Eight years, two pregnancies—easy pregnancies,
mostly, but what was "easy" about producing a human
being in your uterus, for chrissakes?—and who knows
how many dirty diaper changes later, she had lost her
sense of who she was.

As she drove south on Oxford, she wondered if she was
a bad mother or merely being honest. At Channing, she
waited while a herd of slow-moving undergraduate students migrated north for their morning classes. Several
years before, she had seen Janis Joplin in concert in San
Francisco. Midway through a song, Janis had taken a swig
out of a bottle of Jack Daniel's and then she had kept right
on singing. As my mother turned left, she ached to undo
her life—to unmarry herself, to unimpregnate herself,
to unbecome who she had become. The pain was like an
icepick in her sternum.

Atherton was congested with cars. She parked around
the corner, pulled me from the back seat, and dragged me
down the block at a fast trot, ducking her head to avoid
the low branches of the massive oak tree that reached
over the fence at the corner. At the entrance ramp, we
joined the thick processional of other mothers and kids.
(The other fathers were, like my father, at work.)

At the doorway of the west classroom, I stopped.

"C'mon, Sus!" my mother cajoled, straining to sound
upbeat. She had errands to run, books to read, a dissertation to complete. She could not take another second of

subjugating herself to someone else's needs. She stifled a scream.

As I stepped across the threshold, my life was transformed. Unbeknownst to me, I had joined a cohort of over a hundred Berkeley preschoolers who would be studied for the next thirty years in a groundbreaking psychological experiment that would predict who we would grow up to be.

Formally, the psychological experiment in which I was a research subject is known as Block and Block Longitudinal Study, 1969–1999. Colloquially, it's referred to as the Block Study. But our parents, without whose written consent our researchers could not study us, were told it was called the Block Project. (In all likelihood this was designed to put our parents' minds at ease about turning their children into human guinea pigs; anyone who knows anything about science knows that a *project* and a *study* are not the same thing.)

In 1969, married UC Berkeley research psychologists Jack and Jeanne Block set out to answer a straightforward question: If you study a child, can you predict who that child will grow up to be? In the late 1960s, personality psychology was in the midst of a paradigm crisis. In 1968, Walter Mischel, an influential Stanford University psychology professor (today he is perhaps best known for his "marshmallow experiment" studies of delayed gratification in children), had published a new book, *Personality and Assessment*, in which he dismissed personality as a myth. According to personality trait psychologists like the Blocks, human behavior was shaped by personality traits that remained relatively stable over time; therefore, human behavior was predictable. According to Situationists like Mischel, human behavior was shaped by the situation in which an individual found him- or herself; therefore, human behavior was *un*predictable. So who was right?

The Blocks devised a plan to undertake an unprecedented longitudinal study, a type of research design that tracks the same variables over a short or long period of time, that would demonstrate, as William Wordsworth writes in his 1802 poem "My Heart Leaps Up": "The Child is the father of the Man." Across three decades, the couple would follow a cohort of children as their lives unfolded through time, from early childhood and well into adulthood. It would be a Herculean task to study a group of kids from such a young age and for so many years.

At the Child Study Center, we would be selected from three consecutive classes of preschoolers. In addition to being studied at the preschool, we would be assessed at nine key developmental stages: ages three, four, five, seven, eleven, fourteen, eighteen, twenty-three, and thirty-two. In the T-shaped building, the Blocks, our co-principal investigators, and their team of researchers would study us from an observation gallery hidden between the mirror-twin classrooms. In the rectangular building, their team of examiners would assess us individually in testing rooms equipped with one-way mirrors and eavesdropping devices. Our preschool teachers would be solicited for their insights into our personalities. After preschool, we would scatter to the winds, attending different schools. From that point forward, we would be assessed at Tolman Hall, a looming Brutalist concrete structure on the north side of campus that housed the Graduate School of Education in its east tower and the Department of Psychology, where the Block Project was headquartered, in its west tower.

Rarely undertaken, notoriously costly, and difficult to manage, longitudinal studies are the ne plus ultra of scientific research. For the Blocks, a less ambitious study would skim the surface of why people turn out as they do. "If one casts a line only into the shallow waters of a nearby pond, only little fish will be caught," Jack writes in "Venturing a 30-Year Longitudinal Study," an essay about the study that was published in *American Psychologist* in 2006. "To catch the big fish, it is necessary to venture out into deep water."

Over the years, the Blocks would collect what they referred to as "L.O.T.S." of data on us: L-data, which include our *life* history, demographic information, and schooling; O-data, the *observations* of our examiners, parents, and teachers; T-data, the results of the many *tests* we would take (IQ tests, personality tests, galvanic skin response, and more); and S-data, our *self-reported* data (or: what we would disclose in interviews). Our school report cards would be considered. Psychologists would analyze us. At six, we would be studied at home. Assessments would be conducted one-on-one, while interacting with one of our parents, or while interacting with both of our parents. Our mothers and fathers would be asked about their child-rearing strategies, their marriages and divorces, and our relationships with our siblings, if we had any. Our personality traits and characteristics would be quantified and cataloged, among them: our ability to delay gratification, our distractibility, our capacity for curiosity, our interest in risk-taking, our creative expression, our level of ambition, our "moral development," and our egocentrism.

In his essay, Jack described their methods and provided an exhaustive accounting of the many and myriad ways in which we were assessed:

> Thus, we used measures of activity level; delay of gratification; distractibility; vigilance; exploratory behavior; motor inhibition (Simon Says!); susceptibility to priming; satiation and cosatiation; planfulness; curiosity; instrumental behavior when confronted by barriers or frustrations; dual focus (the ability to split attention); susceptibility to perceptual illusions; risk-taking; level of aspiration; utilization of feedback; divergent thinking and other indexes of creativity; chained word association (to index associative drift); various cognitive styles, such as field dependence—independence; reflection—impulsivity; category breadth; perceptual standards; sex-role typing; egocentrism; physiognomic perception; incidental learning; metaphor generation; short-term memory (via digit span); memory for sentences; memory for narrative stories; moral development; skin conductance when lying; skin conductance when startled; recovery rate from startle; the phenomenology of emotions; free play at age 3 and again at age 11 (patterned after Erik Erikson's approach);

self-concept descriptions; decision time and decision confidence in situations varying in the intrinsic difficulty of decision; blood pressure and heart rate in response to a set of stressors; depressive realism; false consensus; and core-conflict relationship themes. We also used the full Wechsler intelligence test at ages 4, 11, and 18; the Raven Progressive Matrices Test; Piagetian measures of conservation; a measure of semantic retrieval; the Lowenfeld Mosaic Test; the Stroop Test; the Kogan Metaphor Test (for metaphor comprehension); Loevinger's sentence-completion measure of ego development; Kelly's Rep Test; the Spivack and Shure Interpersonal Problem-Solving measure; descriptions of ideal self, of mother, of father, and of sought-for love object; enactment of a standard set of expressive situations (videotaped); experience sampling for a week (via a beeper); health indexes; activity and interest indexes; long and intensive clinical interviews (now on DVDs) relating to, among other topics, adult attachment, ways of knowing, and ego development; Diagnostic Interview Schedule screening, so as to connect with the *Diagnostic and Statistical Manual of Mental Disorders* classification system; and hundreds of questionnaire and inventory items relating to a host of personality scales. In assembling and administering this array of procedures, we were continually concerned for the age-appropriateness of the procedures used. We also tried to be attentive to the ongoing psychological literature, introducing into the assessments new topics and au courant measures relevant to our conceptual focus.

"As an observation, not a boast," he asserts of us, their scientific progeny, sounding like a proud father, "it is likely that there is not another sample in psychology so extensively, intensively, protractedly assessed."

———————

In the earliest memory I have from my tenure in the Block Project, I was around four. In preschool, I didn't know that I was in a study. At the Child Study Center, I had no idea that anyone was watching me. At that time, I was wholly unaware that behind the eight-foot-wide screened glassless windows on the east wall of the west classroom there was a long, narrow, dimly lit observation gallery in which one or more researchers was perched on a blue-topped metal stool at a built-in wood desk with task lighting and taking notes on what I was doing.

I had been at the preschool perhaps a few months when one morning I walked past the floor-to-ceiling orange-framed windows on the south side of the classroom through which the sun was streaming and out to the play yard. It was a warm day, as I recall it, and the other kids were running, jumping, screaming, dancing, riding tricycles, and building with blocks. At the stand-up sandbox, I dedicated myself to constructing the tower of a sandcastle with a plastic cup that I had filled with sand that I had made wet at a nearby outdoor faucet. A woman who wasn't my teacher appeared at my side. She squatted so we were eye-to-eye.

"Want to go to the game room?"

I followed her through the classroom, across the walkway, past a sliding glass door, and into the other building. In a small room, I sat at a table that faced the sliding glass door and through which I could see the building from which I had come. ("In this way, children are more comfortable because they can see familiar surroundings from the testing areas," a 2013 application for landmark status from the City of Berkeley for the Child Study Center that was approved the same year explains helpfully.) As she nodded encouragingly, I worked on a puzzle, the shapes of which were farm animals: a horse, a donkey, a pig, and so on. When I had assembled the puzzle, she presented me with a small gift-wrapped box as a prize, the contents of which I can no longer remember.

In the next memory I have of being in the Block Project, I was around six. One afternoon, a woman appeared at the front door of our house. By this time I had graduated from the preschool and was a first grader at an alternative private grade school that I attended alongside kids whose parents had thought it was a good idea to give their children names like Sunshine and Storm. My mother didn't tell me why the woman was there, only that she was going to watch me play. I went upstairs to my bedroom; the woman followed me. Self-consciously, I retrieved a few stuffed animals from the toy chest at the foot of my bed. The woman observed from the doorway while I arranged the animals into a tea party. I laid out my teacups and saucers. Sometimes, she would write something in her notebook. Every once in a while, I would look up at her. She would smile reassuringly. After a while, I forgot that she was there.

In the first memory I have of the Block Project in which I realized not everything was as it seemed, I was around seven or eight. I was sitting at a table in one of the experiment rooms in Tolman Hall, and it was springtime, I think, and a windy day, I believe, as the branches of the redwood tree on the other side of the south-facing window were scraping against the glass, which made it sound as if something was trying to claw its way inside. The room itself was stark and spare. The walls were white or whitish, and the carpet was maybe a grayish-green color, a color that I now associate with rooms through which people pass but do not stay—for example, a doctor's waiting room or the Department of Motor Vehicles.

To the left of the door through which I had entered, there was a black wall phone that didn't have a numbered dial, which struck me as odd, as we had a black wall phone in our kitchen at home, and it had a numbered dial on it; how else were you going to call someone? On the wall opposite me, there was a full-length mirror, taller than it was wide. To the left of the mirror, there was a small hinged opening with a door—roughly two feet tall by two feet wide—by which one could pass something between the rooms and which had an unlit red light next to it, the purpose of which was a mystery.

In the room, there were two people: a man and me. He was tall and gaunt, had a hangdog face, and was wearing gold wire-framed glasses. For some time, he had been asking me questions: what I liked, what I didn't like, how I felt about my parents and my sister, what I wanted to be when I grew up (a veterinarian, I related, since I loved animals, cats especially, of which our family had three). Earlier, someone, not one of my parents, who were busy, had picked me up from school and brought me here. Now it was late in the afternoon.

"Would you like some candy?" he inquired politely.

I eyed the bowl of M&M's on the table between us. It had been hours since I had eaten lunch, and I was starving. My stomach growled its response. But I hesitated. My mother called me *piggy* if I drank too much milk. ("Piggy, piggy, piggy!" she would scold exasperatedly, an almost empty half-gallon of milk in her hand as she stood in front of the refrigerator.) Would he think I was *piggy* if I ate some of his candy? If he did, I might not be able to come back again. And I liked coming here, to these rooms, where I was the center of attention.

At home, I felt invisible. By this point, my mother was an English professor at a small, private college in the East Bay. Both my parents were preoccupied with work: teaching classes, grading papers, securing tenure, and writing books. My sister ignored me, or erected walls of cereal boxes between us on the round wooden table in the breakfast nook because I stared at her too much, or she pulled one of my fingers backward until I cried if I tried to follow her and her girlfriend to the dime store. As a result, I spent a great deal of time alone in my room, playing with my stuffed animals, talking to one of the cats, or scripting and dramatizing complex melodramas for the family that occupied the 1950s two-story tin dollhouse my maternal grandmother had given me. (She lived far away, in Pennsylvania, and we visited her once a year at Christmas. I gathered that my mother didn't like her.)

In Tolman Hall, I felt *seen*. These people wanted to know everything about me: who I was, how I saw the world, what kind of person I wanted to be. When I spoke, they nodded encouragingly. It made me feel how I longed desperately to feel: *special*.

To be safe, I ignored my hunger and shook my head no.

"Oh, I've forgotten that there's something I must do," the man said a little while later. He stood up. "Susannah, you can stay here while I take care of it."

As soon as the door closed behind him, I leaped from my chair and lunged for the candy. Inadvertently, I knocked over the bowl. Horrified, I watched the M&M's bounce wildly across the tabletop. I grabbed several handfuls and stuffed them in my mouth.

Suddenly I froze. In the mirror, I saw, my hot cheeks were bright pink, flushed with embarrassment. (What had caught my attention? A cough? A shadow? A movement?) Someone on the other side was watching me, I surmised, although it would take me years to identify whom.

I grew up in a house that was filled with books. Books were crammed into the built-in shelves in the living room and the bookshelves in the second-floor enclosed porch off the primary bedroom that we referred to as the study, where my father wrote his books; teetered in tall, listing towers on nightstands; sat, half read and seemingly abandoned, in stacks on toilet tanks. My parents read voraciously, widely, across genres: fiction (William Faulkner's *As I Lay Dying*,

Ralph Ellison's *Invisible Man*, Sylvia Plath's *The Bell Jar*); nonfiction (Tom Wolfe's *The Electric Kool-Aid Acid Test*, Virginia Woolf's *A Room of One's Own*, Frederick Douglass's *Narrative of the Life of Frederick Douglass*); poetry (Homer's *The Iliad* and *The Odyssey*, Audre Lorde's *The Black Unicorn*, *The Complete Poems of Emily Dickinson*); essays (Ralph Waldo Emerson's *Self-Reliance*, Joan Didion's *Slouching Towards Bethlehem*, James Baldwin's *Notes of a Native Son*); and memoirs (Maxine Hong Kingston's *The Woman Warrior*, Elie Wiesel's *Night*, Maya Angelou's *I Know Why the Caged Bird Sings*). My father read supine on the living room sofa. My mother read in bed. If neither parent could be located readily, they might be discovered behind a closed bathroom door, reading in the tub or on the can. By the age of nine, I had revised my plan to become a veterinarian and resolved to become a writer of books, hoping I might one day write a book that would command my parents' attention.

My parents had bought the house after I was born. It was light and airy. There were banks of French windows in the living room and brass-handled French doors in the dining room that opened onto a garden with a rock pool surrounded by moss and shadowed by bamboo trees. In the breakfast nook, a bay window overlooked the backyard. The backyard had a lawn, a magnolia tree, a brick patio, a greenhouse, a red wooden playhouse with a slide, and a plum tree with a swing. On the second floor, my parents' bedroom had a view of the Golden Gate, my sister's bedroom had a balcony, and my bedroom had a built-in desk and bookshelf.

In the shared galaxy of my childhood home, my parents

occupied remote planets. They were emotionally distant, neither touchy nor feely, and oftentimes distracted. This was a testament to how they had been raised. My maternal grandparents had led my mother to believe that she was never good enough (when she called her parents to let them know that she had gotten tenure, my maternal grandfather had demanded to know when she was going to make full professor), for which she resented them. My paternal grandfather, a minor-league outfielder turned Western Union accountant, died of a heart attack on the floor of a New York City subway train at the age of forty-nine. My father was seventeen and had graduated from Brooklyn Preparatory High School two weeks before. In 1994, my father wrote an essay for *The New York Times Book Review* about why he had spent eight years researching and writing a nearly 600-page biography of Mark Rothko, the famous dead abstract expressionist painter of luminous rectangles. In that essay, my father depicted his own father as a raging alcoholic. He is at least part of the reason why my father was leery of emotional intimacy.

My sister's response to our upbringing was to absent herself. She spent most of her time riding horses at an equestrian stable in Tilden Park. And I, not unlike the titular character of Antoine de Saint-Exupéry's 1943 novella *The Little Prince*, a copy of which sat on my bookshelf, inhabited my own planet. Planet Susannah, population: one.

Books offered the tantalizing possibility of bridging the distance between my parents and me. Because my parents loved books, I learned to love them too, the way one might learn to love a sibling. At the North Branch of the

Berkeley Public Library, my mother permitted me to check out any book I wanted. On Telegraph Avenue, my father escorted me down sidewalks crowded with stressed-out students, harried professors, and drugged-out hippies to Moe's Books and Cody's Books.

When my father ensconced himself in the study to write his second book, I watched from the other side of the French doors, my forehead pressed against the cool glass, as he pecked at the typewriter keys with his forefingers. Crumpled balls of paper upon which he had typed something that had dissatisfied him gathered at his feet like a snowdrift. Around this time, my mother became more withdrawn. Her lips formed a thin line of disappointment, at what I didn't know; her narrowed eyes drifted off mid-conversation to gaze out the window, at what I couldn't see; her long arms folded protectively over her chest, as if warding off an anticipated blow from an unseen enemy from which I could not protect her.

One night, when I was around nine, my parents' fighting woke me. In my bare feet, I tiptoed to the top of the staircase. I slid to my knees, my floral-patterned flannel nightgown pooling on the floor around me. I wrapped my fingers around the spindles of the wooden banister. I couldn't make out any words. My father was angry. My mother was crying.

I retreated to my bedroom. I flipped on the light. Looking for something to distract me from what I had witnessed, I scanned the titles on my bookshelf: Frances Hodgson Burnett's *The Secret Garden*, C. S. Lewis's *The Lion, the Witch, and the Wardrobe*, Tove Jansson's *Finn Family*

Moomintroll. Between their covers, I was transported into fantastical universes: where a neglected girl met a special friend in a secret garden, where beavers spoke and fauns were real, where a family of furry white beings that resembled small hippopotami and walked upright on their hind legs carried out familial adventures from which they always returned home safe.

I grabbed my favorite book: *Mrs. Frisby and the Rats of NIMH.* Awarded the John Newbery Medal in 1972, the year after it was first published, and written by Robert C. O'Brien, it concerns itself with a widowed mother mouse who sets out on a perilous journey to save her sick son. Along the way, she meets a mischief of rats that escaped from a research laboratory where a scientific experiment funded by a mysterious entity called NIMH turned them into geniuses.

The curious tale was based in truth. In the early 1960s, while reporting a story, O'Brien (an editor and writer for *National Geographic*) had visited the Maryland laboratory of a National Institute of Mental Health—or NIMH— researcher, John B. Calhoun, who was studying overpopulation in rodents. In a large pen that Calhoun called a mouse universe, the population had exploded, and what he had christened the behavioral sink had begun. The mothers were eating their young. The males nicknamed the beautiful ones were self-grooming obsessively. The group had devolved into "sexual deviation" and cannibalism.

I read the book under my quilt with a flashlight, the white fancy rat my parents had given me for my birthday sleeping soundly in its wood shavings nest in a wire-mesh cage I kept atop my desk. I had no idea the NIMH that had experimented on my beloved book's genius rats was named for the very same federal agency that was funding the study that was studying me.

In my life, fact and fiction were one and the same.

TWO

On the day my father left my mother, I came home from school to a silent house. My mother was at work; my sister was riding horses. In the living room I dumped my backpack on the mustard-colored carpet, walked past the Steinway piano that my mother played less frequently, and flipped on the television set to keep myself company. A group of kids on a show I liked to watch called *Zoom* sang as they bounded around while gesticulating enthusiastically. I sang along under my breath as I attempted to mirror their movements. As I spun around, I realized something was different. There were empty spaces on the bookshelves where, my mother would explain, my father's books had been. I climbed onto the sofa and stood unsteadily on the squishy seat cushion. Holding on to the back of the sofa with one hand, I stuck my other hand into the gaps between the books. My fingers opened and closed, grasping at nothing.

It wasn't like I hadn't seen the signs. But I was eleven, so I hadn't known how to read them. The more frequent late-night fighting. The morning I discovered my father in a sleeping bag on the sofa. The time we were driving to King Tsin, a Chinese restaurant on Solano Avenue, my parents in the front seat and my sister and me in the back, and I leaned over the seats and, apropos of nothing, asked my parents if they were going to get a divorce. My mother responded in the negative, and my father said nothing. His hands were wrapped tightly around the steering wheel, I had noticed, the white of his knucklebones pressing against the taut skin.

"Your father and I are divorcing," my mother had announced at the kitchen table not long after that. My father had squirmed uncomfortably in his chair, looking like he wanted to be anywhere but there. I had wanted to cry, but I could hear my sister's voice in my head: *You're such a crybaby!* So I had swallowed my tears. "Do you have any questions?" my mother had asked impatiently. I shook my head no. My mother sighed. My father stared out the window. I slipped off my chair and retreated upstairs to my bedroom. At my desk, I had opened the oversize notebook in which I recounted the day's events and written: *Mom and Dad are getting a divorce.* Now what was happening was no longer inside me, which seemed preferable.

I jumped off the sofa, leaving the emptied bookshelves behind me. I bounded up the stairs to my bedroom. By this time, my pet rat and its cage were gone. One day when I was at school, my mother had left my bedroom door open by accident. Our white cat had leaped onto the desk and knocked over the cage while attempting to extract the rat for a snack. The little bones of the rat's neck had broken in the fall, my mother had told me, killing it instantly.

I walked over to my dollhouse. I dropped to my knees and perused the interior. I was too big to play with dollhouses anymore, I had decided, and the floors were gathering dust. The mother was in the bathtub, fully dressed. The daughter was sprawled on the kitchen floor, the upper half of her body and her head under the breakfast table. A plastic donkey in a straw hat was grazing on the primary bedroom carpet. The father was in the living room. I had wanted to sit him in one of the armchairs, so he could read a miniature book, but his limbs didn't bend, so I had stood him near the door, as if he was preparing to exit. I plucked out the father, opened a drawer, and put him in it.

In my twin bed, I pulled the pink-and-purple Amish quilt with a star on it that my grandmother had given me over my head. I closed my eyes and imagined I was standing at the end of a hallway lined with doors that led to rooms. I had been here before. This was the place where I put all the things I was feeling that I didn't want to feel: sad, alone, invisible. One by one, I opened the doors and put the bad feelings in the rooms behind the doors and closed the doors. Afterward, I felt better, which is to say, I felt nothing.

Not long after my father moved out, I was sitting in class at my grade school. On the east side of the room, the school secretary, whose glasses hung on a chain and who had a complicated updo, appeared in the doorway. She scanned the room.

"Susannah, come with me, please."

The other kids turned to look at me, their expressions a mix of curiosity (*where is she going?*) and envy (*why does she get to leave math class?*). As I followed the secretary out the door, my face flushed a little. I was embarrassed to have been singled out, but I was also pleased by the attention I was getting.

At the school's main entrance, a man greeted me. He led me to a recreational vehicle parked at the curb. To me it looked like an ordinary RV. In actuality, this was a "mobile laboratory" that the Block Project used so they could assess us at our schools and outside our homes. (Jack had laid the carpeting, and Jeanne had hung the curtains she'd sewn.)

I climbed up the steps and took a seat at a small table in the main cabin. It was time to play a game, the man said. He placed a stiff piece of thick paper on the table in front of me. I looked at the paper. There was a picture on it— although it wasn't really a picture, or not a very good one. It looked like someone had spilled ink. (This was a Rorschach ink blot test, which was developed in 1921 and is a way of assessing personality characteristics and diagnosing mental health disorders.)

"What could this be?" the man said.

"Two clowns in hats clapping," I said.

He placed another picture in front of me.

"What could this be?"

"A monster in a fur coat."

He put another picture in front of me.

"What could this be?"

"A bat about to eat me."

A look of amusement flickered across his face. I hoped I was giving him the right answers. If I did, maybe he would tell my mother how smart I was.

(In the rear of the RV, the other examiner, who was hiding in a concealed compartment in order to spy on me through the one-way mirror in the door without my detecting it, adjusted their position in the cramped space.)

By the time I returned to the classroom, the school day was almost over. I slid back into my chair. The teacher was talking, but my brain felt fuzzy. The games, the questions, the time I had spent in the RV had made me tired.

"Where did you *go*?" my best friend queried. She poked me in the side. Her blue eyes were wide with curiosity. "What were you *doing*?"

I shook my head and smiled conspiratorially. I was in a secret club for special kids, and she wasn't. I scanned the classroom. Were any of the other kids in the same secret club? One boy was drawing a stick figure on the chalkboard. His dad worked with my dad. Maybe he was in the secret club, too.

When the carpool dropped me off after school, I saw my mother's car in the driveway. I hurried inside to tell her about the man in the RV. She was in the primary bedroom. I stopped in the doorway. She was sitting on the edge of the bed. Her shoulders were hunched. Her face was in her hands.

"Mom?"

She didn't move.

"What's wrong?"

"I'm just…*sad*."

I didn't have to ask why. I went back downstairs and turned on the TV. I lay on the sofa and closed my eyes. As the TV chattered in the background, I returned to the hallway in my mind, disappearing inside myself to the place where I felt nothing at all.

———

At first, my father stayed at UC Berkeley's Faculty Club. A few months later, he moved into an apartment where my sister and I shared a bedroom and that had cockroaches but was near enough to campus that he could walk to work. My mother retreated into a deep depression. My sister rode horses or hung out with her friends. Initially, my father took pains to maintain a close relationship with me: We went roller-skating in San Francisco's Golden Gate Park; had cheeseburgers and ice cream sundaes at Edy's, a Berkeley diner; saw *Escape from Alcatraz* starring Clint Eastwood at the downtown movie theater. My parents had joint custody, so my sister and I spent part of the week at my mother's house and part of the week at my father's place. Eventually my father rented a house in the Berkeley flatlands, where I had my own bedroom and a pet hamster that bit me so often I named him Jaws, after the movie.

When I was around twelve, my father met the woman who would become my stepmother. She was considerably younger than him, had grown up in a wealthy enclave south of San Francisco, and was a poet and a painter. I didn't like her. It seemed to me that her interest was in my father, not his children. My father ceased doing things with him and me and started including her. In this, she felt to me like a wedge between my father and me. Then my father informed me they were getting married. For his betrayal, I boycotted their wedding.

"He only married her for her *money!*" my mother pronounced. That my father had moved on enraged her, and she saw no point in concealing her resentment in front of us. Adding insult to injury, my father and stepmother had bought a house a few miles from her house. The grocery store where my mother bought her vegetables was across the street from their house. Instead of shopping elsewhere, she endured the risk of potentially running into her ex and his wife while bagging her zucchini. I, sensing my mother needed emotional caregiving, became her caretaker, a dynamic known as parentification. Out of solidarity with her, I launched a campaign against my stepmother. At my father's house, I stewed with resentment. I called my stepmother a scumbag. I rolled my eyes when she spoke. Or I pretended she didn't exist.

At thirteen, I transferred from my private school to a public school for the eighth grade. On the first day, I stood on the playground at lunchtime and scanned the cliques. I locked eyes with a girl who had attended my private school—her group was the Preps: the boys in Izod shirts and Topsiders, the girls in Fair Isle sweaters and penny loafers—but she turned away, as if she didn't know me. In the school bathroom, I looked in the mirror. No wonder she had acted that way. My forehead and chin were dotted with zits. I had attempted to tame my curly brown hair with barrettes, but it hadn't worked. I raised my arms to fix my hair, and the armpits of my gray shirt were soaked with sweat. I sniffed my pits. *Pew.* I stank. Worst of all, I was taller than the boys. My feminist mother didn't care about makeup or fashion, and she was so depressed she had forgotten to explain the birds and the bees to me. (I had learned about sex from my sister's well-worn copy of Judy Blume's *Forever.*) I didn't know how to be a *girl.*

That year I did end up making friends with a group of smart, bookish, and nerdy girls. For the ninth grade, we switched to a small campus on University Avenue. It was around this time, when I was fourteen, that I heard from the Block Project again. One day after school, I sat opposite a woman with dirty-blond hair in a Tolman Hall experiment room. At first, her questions were more general. Over time, her probing got more personal. She wanted to know about my parents' divorce (it sucked), if I was happy or unhappy (it depended on the day, really), whether or not I was smoking weed or doing other drugs (no, or not yet, anyway). At the end, she gave me a "beeper." For a week or so, every time the beeper beeped, I punched in a number that represented my mood, per her instructions. While I didn't realize it, I had experienced or was about to experience many of the very life factors in which my researchers were interested: drugs, divorce, and depression. In other words, I was the perfect lab rat.

In the tenth grade, I went to Berkeley High School. One lunch, I sat on a brick bench in the quad eating spicy fries I had bought at the cafeteria, staring at the girls across from me. At home, I pored over fashion magazines—*Vogue, Mademoiselle, Teen*—studying the way the perfect models on the glossy pages applied their makeup, the clothes they wore, how they tilted their heads and half smiled as if they were hearing something super interesting.

These girls on the quad weren't like those models—and they weren't like my girlfriends. These girls had a bad reputation. The Sluts. That's what other people called them. There was something dangerous and powerful about these girls. I admired their Sun-In-lightened short hair gelled into spikes; their shirts, sliced up with scissors, like Madonna's, that exposed their smooth, tanned skin; the silky Dolphin shorts that revealed their butts if they bent over; their sparkling rhinestone earrings; their heavy-handed makeup: layers of lip gloss and thick black eye pencil. The senior boys liked them too, I noticed. I wanted to be liked the way these girls were liked, to be wanted by those older boys. I yearned to be alluring, beguiling, mysterious. These girls were wild, out of control, did not give a *fuck*. They wielded their burgeoning sexuality like a weapon.

"Want to go to a frat party with us this Friday night?" The one with the dark hair had seen me gawking at them. Instead of looking away, she had beckoned me over.

"Totally!" I said, barely able to contain my excitement. Maybe she saw something in me that I couldn't yet see—that, like them, I was lonely, a little sad, hungry for attention.

"Don't get *raped*, you morons," the older brother of the girl with the dark hair sneered as we tumbled out of his car and onto frat row, south of the UC Berkeley campus that Friday night. The sidewalk was thick with college students, the front doors of the frat houses vomiting streams of drunken party-hoppers. I had told my mother that I was going to spend the night at a friend's house. After school let out, we had convened at the house of the dark-haired girl. Her parents weren't home. (They were never home, I would discover.)

"I'm so drunk!" the other girl in our newly formed trio, who had short brown hair, hazel eyes, and the body of a *Sports Illustrated* swimsuit model, had crowed before we left. Madonna had pranced around on the TV screen. Who knows how many shots of vodka we'd had.

"Want to try?" I had turned away from Madonna to find the dark-haired girl standing behind me in the living room. She had opened her palm, revealing three white pills, one for each of us. "It's Ecstasy." *No backing out now.* I had downed one.

In the car, we had smoked a joint in the back seat.

On the sidewalk, I bent over to check my lip gloss in the window of a parked car. My eyes were rimmed with kohl eyeliner, my hair was stiffly coiffed with gel, my rhinestone earrings were dangling from my earlobes, my cut-up pink shirt was slipping off one shoulder, and my jeans were tighter than tight. Off balance, I stumbled forward and fell onto my hands and knees. The other girls burst into laughter, and I laughed too. The world was spinning around me, moving faster than I could keep up with, gyrating out of control.

"Let's go!" Our fearless leader grinned as she pulled me up by the hand. Her pupils were like saucers; were mine too? She headed up the stone stairs to the nearest frat. I trotted after her. We reached the front patio, pressed through the throng and into the frat. As we filled our red plastic Solo cups from the keg of beer, a group of college boys descended on us.

"You're tall." A towering, muscular blond in a Cal football jacket had appeared at my side. "That's hot." I could tell by the way he was looking at me that he had no idea that I was fifteen. People thought I was older because I was tall. Casually, he looped his arm around my waist. I leaned into him, figuring that would stop me from falling over again. "Want to see my room?" he whispered wetly in my ear. Before I could answer, he grabbed my hand, drawing me upstairs. In his dimly lit room, he stuck his tongue in my mouth. He pulled me down on top of him on his twin bed. He stripped off my clothes. He climbed on top of me. His boozy breath was hot on my neck. I lay on my back, staring at the ceiling, as he buried his face between my legs.

I feel nothing, I thought, and closed my eyes.

The next morning, he dropped me off at my girlfriend's house. I never heard from him after that. I told myself it didn't really matter. A guy had wanted me, if only for one night.

I can't remember when or how or from whom, but at some point I had learned that I was a subject in a longitudinal study. The so-called secret club I had imagined had a name. It had other members, who were kids, like me. And it was important. It was the reason I had played those games with strangers at the preschool, answered those questions at Tolman Hall, scrutinized those inkblots in the RV. My associations with these every-several-years assessments, comprising hours and hours of sessions, were by and large positive (even if sometimes afterward I felt mentally exhausted). When I was little, I liked the attention. As I got older, an idea formed in my head: I was part of something bigger than I was.

You might think that if you were a research subject it would change your life, that being in a study would shape who you were, that because you were being observed you would be compelled to become a better version of yourself than you might have otherwise. And all of that might be true. But at the same time, it might cause you to feel a great deal of internal pressure to be exceptional, to be more than who you were, to perform well inside the bell jar under which you were trapped. Or perhaps both of these things could be true simultaneously: an increased sense of your potential and the simmering terror that you might fail to fulfill it.

"You look like a *dude*."

It was a chilly spring day, and I was sitting in the back row of my sophomore biology class. That morning I had donned a black coat I'd bought secondhand and a plaid collared shirt like some of the other girls were wearing, a style inspired by Boy George. On other girls, it looked cool. But I was taller—at sixteen, I was five-foot-ten—and had broader shoulders. Since the first grade, boys had been making fun of me for my size, saying I looked like a guy. I was *sick* of it.

"You look like a *bitch*," I shot back.

He half turned and squeezed the juice box he was drinking. Purple grape juice shot out of the straw and sprayed all over my clothes.

Rage overtook me. I stood up and slapped the tall, lanky Berkeley High basketball player as hard as I could across the back of his head.

"You *cunt!*" he screamed.

I ducked as he scrambled up and took a swipe at the side of my head. I was too slow. His open-handed blow struck my left ear. My eardrum shrieked.

"Not in my class!" the teacher yelled. We ignored him.

"Get the fuck away from me!" I hollered. I backed down the aisle between the desks. The basketball player pursued me, swinging lefts and rights. I didn't know what else to do. I kicked him, landing a glancing blow to his nuts.

Someone grabbed me from behind. Someone else grabbed him from behind. I struggled, trying to free myself. I wanted to hit him again.

"You're lucky I'm not expelling you, Miss Breslin." The head of security shook his head, disgusted. He stroked his goatee. He wrote something on his report. "Suspension. For one week. And no more fighting."

"If you keep acting like this," my mother said as she drove me home, "I will *send you away.*" She was staring straight ahead with her chin jutted out, like she did when she was mad. I crossed my arms defiantly and watched the houses whiz past. The fistfight in biology was the least of it.

If you only knew. All the boys. All the drugs. All the supposed sleepovers when I was creeping around the Bay Area, speeding across the Bay Bridge high on however many hits of Ecstasy, or buzzed on however many lines of speed or coke, or drunk on however many shots of vodka or gin or Mad Dog, to dance into the early hours at a nightclub I got into with my fake ID; going to more frat parties to disappear into more rooms with more college guys whose names I couldn't remember, who were sometimes in their early twenties, who, for all I knew, were my father's students; and my grades on my next report card that, thanks to all the homework I wasn't doing and classes I was skipping, would slip from A's and B's to D's and F's.

Still, what my mother said scared me. If she kicked me out, I couldn't go to my father's. He had told me that if I wasn't nicer to my stepmother, I couldn't stay at his house anymore, so I had stopped going over there. It seemed he didn't want me around either.

When we got home, I slammed the car door, marched upstairs, and slammed my bedroom door. Dirty clothes were strewn all over the floor. Smears of black mascara, turquoise eye shadow, and hot-pink lipstick stained my desk. One wall was covered with the pages I had torn from the magazines featuring the beautiful women I wanted to become. I sat down on the bed. I crawled under the covers. I curled up into a ball.

For some reason, I thought about the Block Project. I wondered what they would think of me. Technically, the study didn't intercede in my life. Nevertheless, it would resurface in my head when I needed it most. *They* thought I was special. *They* thought I was worthy. *They* believed in me. Didn't they? I did not feel special now. I felt…*un*special. I buried my head in my pillow and started sobbing. Something had to change. Me, probably.

By my junior year, I had disentangled myself from the bad girls, stopped partying, and gone back hanging out with my nerdy girlfriends. Over the summer, I had taken two summer school classes at UC Berkeley to make up for the classes I had flunked as a sophomore. Midway through my junior year, I transferred from Berkeley High to the Urban School of San Francisco, a private high school in the Haight-Ashbury district, the home of the Summer of Love in 1967. My classmates included the daughters of Alice Walker, Nancy Pelosi, and Barbara Boxer, and a son of a Getty. The curriculum was divided into semesters. The classes had a dozen students. In the main building, the indoor courtyard had a tree growing in the middle of it.

In the fall of my senior year, I started applying to colleges. My future was coming into focus, like a Polaroid picture. One morning, I went to a building in San Francisco to attend an immediate decision admissions program for Bard College, a private liberal arts college in Annandale-on-Hudson, New York. At the end of a full day of interviews, I had an offer to attend Bard. I had to let them know by May 1 if I was going to accept it. Afterward, I stood on the sidewalk, panicking. I couldn't breathe. My palms were slick with sweat. My head was spinning. Was I as smart as they seemed to think I was, or was I an imposter?

Was I becoming the person I wanted to be, or was I becoming the person everyone else thought I should be?

Phony. Fake. Fraud. The voices in my head grew louder as the months passed. I couldn't tell my parents about my crisis of confidence; for the first time in a long time they seemed like they were proud of me. I stopped going to my classes. I didn't want to feel this paralyzing terror, so I reconnected with the hard-partying girls, got high, and forgot about everything. I went to their Berkeley High prom, bombed. By April, I had dropped out of school.

"What is wrong with you?" my mother wailed in the living room.

"I'm really disappointed in you," my father opined on the telephone.

That month, my stepmother gave birth to their daughter. It was official: My father had a new family, and I wasn't part of it. It seemed as if I had been replaced altogether.

Around this time, when I was eighteen, a letter—it was always a letter, and you never knew when you would get one—from the Block Project arrived, asking if I would come to Tolman Hall for my latest assessment. In the dining room, I held the letter in one hand and the envelope in the other. Maybe talking to them could help me decide what I was going to do next with my life. *Maybe they know me better than I know myself.*

"What are your morals?" the examiner asked as we sat in the experiment room on a swelteringly hot day. I racked my brain, but I couldn't recall my parents having broached the subject. My upbringing had been free-range, feral, unmonitored. I had run wild in the streets, stayed out late when my age was in the single digits, lived a secret child's life of freedom and self-determination. At a party my parents had thrown when they were married, my sister had cajoled one of the professors into lighting his hair on fire with his cigarette, for our amusement. I could still smell the odor of his burning hair, could still see him grinning as he patted out the flames with the palm of his hand. While my mother had shopped at the grocery store, I had floated over to the books section to peruse counterculture comic books featuring the artistry of Robert Crumb, impressed by the oversize boobs and butts of the barely clad women, absorbing the relentless perversions of Mr. Natural. Morals? My parents had skipped those.

"I don't have any?" I suggested tentatively.

The examiner made a mark on his paper.

That fall, my mother had a one-year academic appointment at the University of Hawaii. She seemed relieved to be done with raising her children. Since she had rented our house to a family, I moved in with a girlfriend who was obsessed with taking karate classes in a rough part of West Berkeley. I went to a karate class with her and got hooked too. I bought a gi, learned how to break a board with a swift chop, yelled at the top of my lungs while delivering a roundhouse kick. For the first time, I started to feel strong, powerful, in control.

To pay for karate, I got a job making sandwiches and salads at a busy restaurant on Telegraph Avenue. The following year, I enrolled in a community college, where I met a guy who had gone to Berkeley High at the same time I had, and we started dating. After a while, I moved in with him. I took an English lit class and started thinking that maybe I would become an English professor, like my parents. I took a creative writing class and started thinking that maybe I would become a fiction writer, like Faulkner or Hemingway. I took a journalism class and started thinking that maybe I would become a journalist, like Woodward or Bernstein.

When I was twenty-three I heard from the Block Project again. That fall, I would transfer to Cal as a junior, a student at the same university where my father taught, where I had been studied since I was a child. They wanted to assess me. I agreed. I had been their subject for nearly two decades. Plus, there was a financial incentive: a small honorarium.

"Take a look," Jack said, placing a bloated photo album on the table in Tolman Hall. "See if you can find yourself in there." To my ear, he spoke with the same faint Brooklyn accent that my father did. Like me, he had a diastema—a gap—between his two front teeth.

In 1981, I knew, halfway through the study, Jeanne, his beloved wife, with whom he had conceived the project and who had been his co-principal investigator, had died, of pancreatic cancer, at fifty-eight. They had been a matched set: short and gray-haired. In Jack's office, it seemed, Jeanne was not so much gone as a lingering shadowy presence.

I had spent the last few weeks coming and going from Tolman Hall for the assessments. This was my final reward: a meet-and-greet with him.

"This is amazing." I flipped through the pages. The album was filled with photos taken of us when we were preschoolers at the Child Study Center, where the Blocks had gathered their cohort. We were three and four years old, all Berkeley kids, boys and girls, white kids and Black kids and Latino kids and Asian kids, playing and posing and making faces for whoever had been behind the camera. I scanned the photos, some faded from the two decades that had passed, searching for myself.

There I was. I recognized the bangs and the dimples. Then I laughed. For some reason I was topless. I must have stripped off my shirt while playing. The photo had been taken in one of the outdoor play yards. I was in a laundry basket, pushing myself upward and out of it. I was grinning from ear to ear. I looked *happy*—really, truly, completely happy.

"And this is for you." Proudly, Jack presented me with a folder of the published papers he and the other researchers had written about us. I had received some of these a few years before. I had scanned their polysyllabic titles and skimmed their dense prose, but I hadn't studied them closely. It wasn't like reading a personal diary or watching a home movie. It was more like viewing a documentary of your life narrated in a different language.

I closed the album. As we said our goodbyes, my gaze drifted past his shoulder to the filing cabinets. What was in them? Perhaps they held our files. I wished I could open one of the drawers, scan the tabs, withdraw my own file. What would its contents reveal?

By the first day of classes in August, I had broken up with my boyfriend and moved into a house near the Berkeley-Oakland border that I shared with three other female undergrads. With time, my father and I would reconnect, I would develop a relationship with my half sister, and I would learn to tolerate my stepmother. My mother would return from Hawaii. My older sister would move in with her boyfriend, who lived north of the Bay Area, and I would see her every so often. Two years later, my father would beam as he handed me my diploma when I walked across the stage at my graduation ceremony at The William Randolph Hearst Greek Theatre.

Finally, I would be on my way to becoming who I was supposed to be.

In the fall of 1993, I drove from the Bay Area to Chicago to attend the University of Illinois Chicago Program for Writers. For the next almost two years, I studied literature and wrote fiction. By the time I graduated, I still hadn't decided what kind of writer I wanted to be. Ten days after my graduation ceremony, I drove back to the Bay Area. I rented a studio apartment in a Tudor Revival–style building near Oakland's Lake Merritt that I shared with Kurtis, a truculent, obese tomcat I had adopted from an animal shelter in Chicago. To pay the bills, I drove to and from various community colleges, where I taught freshman composition.

Occasionally, I drove past Tolman Hall, wondering when I would hear from them again. Sometimes I would mention to someone in the course of a conversation that I was a subject in a study, and they would ask me what that was like, and I would shake my head, figuring they wouldn't understand. To other people, it was strange, but to me it was perfectly normal that I had grown up under a microscope. Occasionally, I would wonder about the other kids who were in the study. Where were they now? Did they feel the same way I did about it?

Then, on January 6, 1996, my telephone rang late at night. Half-asleep, I sat up in bed, debating whether to get out of bed or let my answering machine pick it up for me. I threw back the covers. In the dark, I fumbled around for the wireless receiver of my landline.

"Hello?"

"Your father is dead," my stepmother informed me.

"No, he's not," I retorted as if words could undo what had happened.

"Yes, he is," she reiterated, as if I hadn't heard her correctly. He had had a heart attack on the living room sofa, she explained. She called the firefighters, but it had been too late. My father was dead, at age sixty.

"You should come and see him," she said.

In my mind's eye, I saw my father's body sprawled on their pale-pink living room carpet. As I tried to figure out what to do, a story my mother had told me popped into my head. Before I was born my parents had gone to a party. My father had gotten drunk. Out of the blue, he had announced: *I'm a tree!* Then he had fallen straight over, like a felled redwood in a forest. This was like that, only he would never be getting back up again.

He wouldn't want me to see him like that. Arguably, I reminded myself, it no longer mattered what my father wanted, seeing as he was dead. *I don't care what my funeral is like because I'll be dead!* he had joked only a few months ago. Despite what he had or had not wanted, I knew *I* didn't want to see him like that. I could never unsee it.

"I don't think so," I said and hung up the phone.

I sat down on the edge of the bed. My relationship with my father had never been the same after he left my mother. Then he had married my stepmother, and it had gotten worse. We had reconnected, but we'd never been as close as when I was little. He was the one who had made me feel loved, as he had knelt next to my bed making up bedtime stories, held my hand while he had helped me find a book I had wanted at Moe's, or wrestled with me on the living room carpet. Now one thing was crystal clear, although it was too late to do anything about it: Having a father who was alive and imperfect was infinitely better than having a dead father. There would be no new versions of our relationship. This was terminal.

How could he be dead? It was impossible to comprehend. He was planning to write a biography of the jazz saxophonist John Coltrane. Now that book would never be written. There would be no more books from my father. When I was little, he used to make me laugh, and I would yell, "No more jokes!" There would be no more dad jokes either.

A few weeks later, his memorial service was held at the Hillside Club, a North Berkeley social club that dates to the early twentieth century. In the front row, I sat next to my older sister, my half sister, and my stepmother. ("*I* was married to him longer than *she* was," my mother had sniffed resentfully of my stepmother, having been relegated to a row behind us.)

When it was my turn to speak, I joked that it was too bad my father wasn't in attendance because he would have enjoyed listening to people praising him for two hours. People laughed. After I read what I had written, an English professor who in a few months would be named the 8th Poet Laureate Consultant in Poetry to the Library of Congress approached me and told me how moved he had been by my words. Mostly, I had thought of my father as the writer. *Maybe I don't have to figure out what kind of writer I am,* I thought. *Maybe I am one.*

A few weeks later, my stepmother called me again. Per my father's wishes, his body had been cremated. Did I want some of his *cremains*, she wanted to know, using the term for what's left behind after something is cremated.

The next day, I went to their house. A shoebox-size box in a burgundy velvet drawstring sack sat on the dining room table. It was bigger than I had expected; that made sense, because my father had been so tall. I removed the box from the sack, pried open the lid, and peered inside. Thick gray dust was littered with shards of bone. Using a teaspoon, I scooped several shovelfuls into a sandwich-size Ziploc bag. I secured the top with a twist tie.

"Look who's here!" I said when I went to my mother's house afterward. I held up the bag as I stood on her porch. My mother cackled. In the kitchen, she handed me a wooden box that had once held peach tea. I placed the bag of what was left of my father in the box and slid closed the lid on his miniature coffin. My father was gone. My father was a ghost.

THREE

I *don't want to be a mother anymore.* I wish I could pinpoint the first time my mother said those words, draw the scene in the kitchen or in her bedroom or driving in the car, wherever it took place, resurrect how it made me feel, a kind of electric shock or a grim acknowledgment or a vale of nothingness, transcribe the dialogue before and after that statement—if it had been prompted by something I had done or if she had been in a particularly dour mood or if she had just spoken it out of thin air—but I can't. That may be because there wasn't a single before and after. There was a time in my life, quite early on, when I sensed my mother did not want to be a mother. And then there was a time in my life when she started saying out loud what I had suspected was true all along. Either way, it was always there.

According to a friend of my father's (another English professor, as all his close friends were) whom I talked to after he died, my father and I had a close bond when I was a child. I can see it in photos from those years. In one, I am tucked cozily into the right side of him as we sit on the living room sofa, the sun streaming in through the window behind us. In another, I am perched next to him on a wood bench near the cabin we had rented in Mendocino one summer so he could work on his latest book, and he is holding the banjo that he was learning to play. In a third, I am standing at his side in the driveway with my arm wrapped around one of his legs, as if willing him not to go, or having intuited he might one day leave me behind.

With my mother, there was a sense of separation from the start. I experienced no similar connection with her, only an overwhelming sense of an absence that had to be navigated, an untraversable distance between us. Motherhood was something from which my mother seemed to want to recuse herself, as if a child was a chore to be done, a task to be dismissed, a box to be checked. Over time, I started to suspect she was harboring a secret. In the closet of her bedroom, she kept a locked metal box of her journals. She wrote in them regularly and had directed a friend to destroy them in the event of her death. In the closet, I stared up at the box, wondering what she had written that had necessitated they be kept under lock and key.

Perhaps my mother's struggle with mothering was due to her mother (for example: When my grandmother wanted my mother to nap, she hit my mother to make her cry so she would sob herself to sleep). Maybe my mother suffered from narcissistic personality disorder, or avoidant personality disorder, or some other type of personality disorder. Regardless of the why, the effect on me as a child was the same. I was starving for affection.

In the absence of my father, the sole source of parental warmth, of any sort of emotional connection or nurturing, I had been left bereft at eleven. In a zombie-like state, I had shuffled through the rest of that school year, and when the summer had arrived, I had slipped into my first depression. I would not get dressed, would not get out of bed, would not do much of anything but stay in my room, reading. Instead of shirts and pants and shoes, I wore a peach nylon nightgown with a brown lace collar that belonged to my mother, like a boudoir version of Miss Havisham, the jilted bride-to-be of Charles Dickens's *Great Expectations*, and went barefoot. When someone came in my bedroom, I pulled the covers over my head and refused to speak. I stopped bathing and brushing my teeth and combing my hair. A rat's nest gathered at the back of my head, and my mother cut the tangled knot out with a pair of scissors.

"I can't believe you let your hair get like this!" she groaned as the strands of hair fell to the bathroom tile at my feet. "You're so *lazy*."

I didn't respond. What was there to say? I *was*.

"How are you feeling?" Dr. Payne had gently pressed her cool stethoscope against my bare chest. I sat upright on the sheet of stiff medical paper she pulled across the examination table, my legs dangling off the side. After a month of my withdrawn state, my mother took me to the pediatrician to determine what was wrong with me, if I had some underlying medical condition that made me not want to do anything, or if I was, as she suspected, merely being dramatic in an attempt to get attention. "Take a deep breath," Dr. Payne said before I could answer. "Good girl. Now put your legs onto the table." I pulled my legs up and stretched them out in front of me. Dr. Payne moved the stethoscope across my back, listening to whatever was going on inside of me. Her touch was comforting. I didn't want Dr. Payne to think I was whatever it was about me that bothered my mother: too *emotional*, too *sensitive*, too *dramatic*.

"Okay, I guess." I shrugged.

Dr. Payne tucked her stethoscope into her pocket. I pulled my knees into my chest and wrapped my arms around my legs, hugging myself. She picked up my file, wrote something in it, closed it.

"You stay here," she said and patted my shoulder. She went to the hallway and closed the door behind her. A few minutes later, she returned with my mother. I dressed as they talked in low tones in a corner of the room. My mother appeared relieved by whatever Dr. Payne was telling her. There was nothing wrong with me, I presumed, as we drove home. Or if there was, no one was telling me what it was. I crossed my fingers, hoping I wasn't sick like the boy my age I'd seen on an after-school special my sister and I had watched, who died. Over the days and weeks and months that followed, my mood improved, and I was more like whoever I had been before. Although sometimes when I looked at my father's empty chair at the breakfast table or at dinnertime, a sadness tugged at me. The depression had abated, but its shadow would remain, lingering on the sidelines.

Nearly two decades later, the depression returned after

my father's death. I could not tolerate, fathom, accept the loss of him from my life. (My mother seemed buoyed that my father had passed. For her, life was a competition, and she had bested him by outliving him. She didn't say it, but I knew what she was thinking: *You're dead, and I'm alive, so I win!*)

That June, as I sat in the passenger seat of a girlfriend's car while we drove across the Bay Bridge to San Francisco, I fantasized about opening the car door, dodging the cars, and throwing myself off the side. That July, I lay in bed, debating whether or not to retrieve a black leather belt with a silver buckle from the closet, wrap it around my neck, balance on my office chair while securing the other end of the belt to the ceiling fan, and then push the chair out from under myself. That August, I examined the indented place where my forearm met my upper arm and wondered how Rothko, the depressive painter who had been my father's literary subject, had felt, having downed a large amount of the antidepressant Sinequan and cut both of his antecubital fossae with a razor blade, as he waited to bleed out. Incrementally, I was sinking, slipping, sliding down into a black hole of dark thoughts and dangerous impulses.

The idea to go to a strip club was mine. It was summertime, over a year after my father's death, and I had quit teaching. As it had turned out, my father had left my sister and me some money. With a financial cushion, I threw myself into becoming a writer, banging out freelance articles for local weeklies and national magazines. The internet was a new-new thing, where you could publish whatever you wanted with little overhead cost, so two girlfriends of mine from graduate school and I launched an online magazine called *The Postfeminist Playground*, where we published essays, fiction, and journalism.

I thought it would be interesting to write about the strip clubs in the North Beach neighborhood of San Francisco. I was curious about these enigmatic clubs on Broadway that I had seen but never entered. As a kid in the back seat of my parents' Dart, I had been driven through San Francisco and spotted The Condor (which, in 1964, became one of the country's first topless bars). Out front, a towering sign featured a supersized blonde, impossibly busty. Her name, I would find out later, was Carol Doda. On the sign, she wore a black bikini with blinking red lights for nipples.

Doda was the opposite of my mother and her friends, who considered makeup, heavily styled hair, and revealing clothes tools the patriarchy used to subjugate and objectify women. But Doda wasn't anyone's tool; she was a legend. She was America's first topless dancer of note, and her surgically enhanced breasts were billed as "the new Twin Peaks of San Francisco." When I was in graduate school, I had seen an episode of HBO's *Real Sex* about strippers, and I was struck by the revelation that strip clubs were places where intimacy was for sale. Sure, it was transient, transactional, and most often conducted between a guy with a handful of dollar bills and a dancer in a G-string and not much else who twirled seductively around a pole on a stage, but there was something *real* about it. The strippers reminded me of the girls I had hung out with in high school, whom everyone else had deemed slutty.

"Oh my god, Susannah, make up your mind!" Anne laughed as we stood at the corner on a Saturday night. Broadway was teeming with drunk guys, sailors on leave, and couples on the prowl for something more interesting than what they had already. I scanned the glowing signs. Roaring 20's. Big Al's. The Hungry I.

"This one!"

We ducked inside.

As we moved down the black hallway toward a red velvet curtain, I worried what someone else in the club might think. I, a woman, was in a strip club. As I pulled back the curtain, it dawned on me that wasn't going to be an issue. There was one thing the men scattered at the small, dimly lit tables around the room were paying attention to, and it wasn't me. It was the half-naked girl on the stage.

Nonchalantly, we took a seat at a table near the back. We ordered a couple of overpriced drinks. I took a sip: It was straight orange juice. The cocktails were alcohol-free, thanks to a California law that prohibited the sale of alcohol in fully nude strip clubs. It didn't matter; my head was buzzing from the drinks we'd had at the bar around the corner.

In one smooth movement, the statuesque brunette dancer teetering on the highest heels I had ever seen peeled off her dental-floss-thin neon-green thong. She tossed the thong to one side, grabbed the pole, climbed up it. High above the crowd, she wrapped her thighs around the pole and bent over backward, throwing her arms open like an inverted angel.

The academic world in which I had grown up was right across the Bay, but it may as well have been a million miles from where I was. I studied a solitary businessman sitting at the next table. His tie was untied. His jacket was slung across the back of his chair. His eyes were glassy. He had been hypnotized. In this world, women had all the power, and men were at their mercy. I didn't want to be a stripper; I was too shy, too insecure, too inhibited to take off my clothes in front of strangers. But I wanted what she had: the stage, the audience in awe, the men gawking at her. As a kid, I had longed for attention. This was an orgy of attention. As a pubescent teen, I was left to figure out my sexuality for myself because my mother was so unhappy. Here, sex was on parade, for sale, everywhere I looked. In the Block Project, I was the object, the one on view, the child studied by researchers from across tables in Tolman Hall's austere experiment rooms. Now I was the voyeur, the looker, the scopophiliac. It was intoxicating.

As we sped back to the East Bay in the early-morning hours, I watched the city get smaller in the side-view mirror. My father was dead, but for a few hours I had forgotten about that. I could write about this. I could be a gonzo journalist, like one of my favorite writers, Hunter S. Thompson, and immerse myself in it. Sex would be my beat.

A month or so later, I opened a copy of a Bay Area weekly and spotted an ad. A porn star named Jenna Jameson was coming to feature dance at the Mitchell Brothers O'Farrell Theatre in San Francisco. At my computer, I Googled the name of the theater. It had a wild backstory, the stuff of perverse legends, and a place in smut history. In

1969, brothers Jim and Artie Mitchell had established the X-rated theater. In 1972, they had released *Behind the Green Door*, as part of the "porno chic" era. Six years ago, Jim had kicked in Artie's door and shot his brother to death, an action for which he had spent the last three years across the Bay's frigid waters at San Quentin State Prison. Was it a sign from the universe that my idol-in-journalism, Hunter S. Thompson, had once been the night manager of what he had proclaimed the "Carnegie Hall of sex in America"? Maybe. Today, thanks to the home video revolution, it was a strip club.

Online, I tracked down an email address for Jameson's publicist. Could I interview her before the show? *Yes* was the response. A week later, I was in a Japantown hotel room, interviewing the closest thing the adult industry had to a crossover star in the making. The baby-faced, blue-eyed bottle blonde answered my questions as she lolled around on the bed with her roadie boyfriend. What struck me wasn't what she said—her claims of female empowerment, her avowed insatiable sexual appetite, her devotion to her legions of fans—but her tiny ankles. Despite all of her big-girl talk, her explicit résumé, and her Jessica Rabbit–like, surgically enhanced dimensions, she was, in the real world, just a girl—a young woman who happened to be on her way to becoming the most famous porn star in the world.

Afterward, as I drove to the theater, it occurred to me that I had stumbled onto something bigger, a story that most people didn't know a lot about: the sex business. It wasn't just about sex or money—although there was plenty of that. It was about desire, longing, and the things people did and said when they thought no one else was looking. Gonzo-journalism-style, I would expose America's seedy underbelly in all its raunchy glory. Along the way, I would be transformed into someone way cooler, more badass, and more fearless than me. I turned onto O'Farrell. The theater's sign was aglow. Right now, I didn't have to think about my father's dead body, my mother's self-interest, or whoever I was "supposed" to be. I could be someone new.

Soon after, I was backstage. In a dressing room, Jameson and Jill Kelly, another porn star and Jameson's onstage costar, were getting ready for the show. I had read about Kelly, who had a long face, blond hair, and a set of red lips tattooed on her well-tanned right butt cheek, in *The New Yorker*. The story mentioned her surfer-dude-turned-porn-star husband, Cal Jammer, who had blown his brains out in front of her home on a rainy afternoon when his career in porn had tanked as hers had soared. A nude Jameson bent over and began coloring in her pubic hair with eye shadow. I admired how unabashed and unashamed she was. *I want to be that shameless.*

Downstairs, the duo stomped out on the stage like oversexed storm troopers in coordinated barely-there costumes and thigh-high platform boots, parading before the appreciative mostly male audience as Marilyn Manson caterwauled about the beautiful people in the background. The men hooted and hollered while the women stripped, revealing gravity-defying breasts with faint half-moon surgical scars underneath them, and spreading their legs for the eager onlookers. For a finale, Kelly did a headstand while Jameson performed—pretended to perform? I wasn't sure—oral sex on her. A slack-faced man gawked at the sexual spectacle as if bearing witness to the Rapture—gobsmacked. I had never had a guy look at me like that. Then again, I had never engaged in girl-on-girl oral sex on a stage in a crowded theater. Was this what guys actually wanted? One girl going down on another girl while everyone watched? It was entirely possible.

When the show was over, the stars posed with their acolytes for $20-a-pop Polaroids. I thought about sitting at a booth, but nude women were lounging on the tabletops, penetrating themselves with dildos, surrounded by men who watched as if they were attending a particularly fascinating fondue party. I pulled out my notebook. A man moved past me, heading to a red-velvet-lined room behind a shimmering gold curtain, led by a scantily clad, be-glittered woman, who, I noticed, smelled like peaches and apricots.

What am I doing here? First strip clubs. Now live sex shows. It was all happening so fast. Still, there was something drawing me forward, pulling me down this path. One day, my descent into the erotic inferno might tell me something about myself too: my own desires, my own secrets, my own longings. I didn't have all the answers…yet.

Outside, two smiling Japanese businessmen greeted Jameson and Kelly. I watched as the foursome slipped into a waiting black stretch limousine and headed for parts unknown. I made my way home. My head was spinning. My thoughts were whirling. My future was beckoning.

———————

I was fifteen the first time I saw a porn movie. It was at the home of one of the girls with whom I would go to frat parties, the girl whose parents were always gone. That afternoon three or four boys showed up at the front door. They were a few years older than us, seniors, and members of a crew that called themselves The Burnies because they smoked weed all the time. One of them had brought the movie. Someone closed the blinds. Someone slipped the VHS tape into the player. Someone pressed PLAY.

John Holmes was the star. A blonde in a blue negligee was his costar. Holmes took off his clothes and with some effort managed to get his enormous penis to half-mast. Then he commenced plowing in and out of the woman. How had he ended up there? How had she ended up there? Did they *want* to be there?

"Look at his cock, bro!" one of the boys marveled.

The girl on the screen moaned. Was she pretending to like it? Or was she into it? It was hard to discern what was real and what wasn't. The truth was there, below the surface, but I couldn't quite grasp it.

"Grosssss!" one of the other girls groaned. She stuck her finger in her mouth, gagging.

"You know you like it," the leader of the boys said. From where he was stretched out on the floor, he reached out and tried to smack her on the ass, but she darted out of the way.

Somewhere in the room in which the man and the woman were boning, there was a camera, recording the action. The actors knew strangers would watch them one day, like we were. So the performers had hidden themselves away, shielding what they were feeling, each playing his or her part. Their expressions were masks they wore for other people, the scrim behind which they concealed their true selves. To my teenage self, it was vaguely familiar, like the adults I knew: mothers and fathers who said one thing and did another, who were there and not there, who disappeared inside themselves.

Over the years that came after, I would occasionally encounter more porn movies, by accident mostly, as a consequence of happenstance or random events. A boy I was seeing would produce one with a flourish. A TV at a house party would be broadcasting one in the background. A marquee of a grimy theater on a San Francisco street would be advertising a porno flick playing on its screen. I was curious, intrigued, titillated. In my mind, porn was a medium for men, a type of movie that existed for the sole purpose of guys jacking off to it, a form of lowbrow cinema that was not to be taken seriously, a punch line to a dirty joke.

When I was in graduate school, my best friend worked at a video store with a cordoned-off section of porn movies. To entertain ourselves, we would rent the titles with the looniest premises: orgy in a barnyard, two guys screwing a double-headed dildo, a filthy send-up of *A Clockwork Orange* titled *A Clockwork Orgy* wherein all the droogs were women. Sometimes I'd find myself asking the same question: *Who are these people, really?*

You would think that when I started writing about sex,

I would have had a clear idea as to why I had chosen that particular subject, but I didn't. You would think that when I went to the O'Farrell Theatre to watch the porn stars perform, I would have had a keen understanding of what I was doing there, but that was not the case. You would think that when, after that night, I couldn't stop thinking about how Porn Valley, where most adult movies were made, was at the other end of the state, I would have had a reasonable explanation as to why I wanted to go there, but you would be wrong. The truth was simple: Were I in Los Angeles, Jenna's publicist had told me, I would be welcome to visit a porn set. No one else was writing about the porn business the way I wanted to do it. A few men, well-known writers among them, had written about the adult industry, parachute journalism, mostly lengthy, leering reports published in men's magazines. A woman could write about porn in a way that a man could not, undistracted, homing in on the humanity in the erotic dream factory. So I went to LA.

On a blisteringly hot late August afternoon in 1997, I found myself on the set of a porn movie titled *Flashpoint*. The plotline, I had been informed, concerned itself with a coterie of male and female firefighters who, after the tragic death of one of their fallen brethren, were consoling one another by engaging in copious amounts of sex. In the middle of the parking lot, somewhere not far from downtown LA, seven people, all porn stars, were having an orgy on a fire truck, not twenty feet away from me.

To my right, the other journalists, a handful of middle-aged men who wrote for magazines with names like

Cheri and *Oui,* took feverish notes. I looked at my notepad; it was blank. I wasn't sure what to write. *Orgy? Fire truck? Sunstroke?*

On the ladder, a blonde was busily fellating her costar. At mid-truck, two men were having a three-way with a different blonde. In the cab, another couple was going at it. In a semicircle, bored crewmembers were watching the performers sweat and pant under the scorching midday sun, the actors pumping and thrusting, their artificially bronzed, shiny skin stretched taut over well-defined abs and manufactured curves. A few yards away, the real firemen, whom I had observed earlier delivering the very real fire truck, which was on loan from the City of Los Angeles for the day, were studying the action as if expecting a test on it at a future date. Overhead, the camera zoomed lazily in and out on a crane, unblinking.

An hour passed as I sweated and took notes I would struggle to decipher later. The performers changed positions. A dog barked in the distance. A plane flew across the cloudless sky. Somebody yawned impolitely. One of the female porn stars groaned. Inner thighs trembled. Missionary became doggie. Woman-on-top became man-on-top. The three-way deconstructed and reassembled into new configurations. The blonde on the ladder appeared to have an orgasm, her high-pitched cry warbling through the industrial area.

Suddenly one of the three-way's woodsmen stepped backward, moving away from the woman bent over in front of him, with whom he had been having sex. He stared down at his flaccid penis in his hand as if it belonged to someone else. Tension filled the air. I held my breath, waiting to see what would happen next.

"Lube!" the woodsman cried like a soldier calling for a medic, and a small bottle sailed across the cloudless sky, landing in his upraised palm with a *smack!* Within minutes, the woodsman had resumed his mechanical plowing. Disaster had been averted. The male journalists seemed relieved.

Two hours after the scene had begun shooting, it was time for the male porn stars to deliver their money shots. To one side of the truck, two crewmembers discussed a "FIP."

"What's a FIP?" I whispered to the nearest porn writer.

"A fake internal pop" was the answer.

The lurking camera hovered in front of the face of one of the three-way's woodsmen, now feigning orgasm for footage that would be intercut in the editing bay with his soon-to-be-delivered money shot. His face contorted. His mouth gaped open. "Oh!" he announced. He looked more pained than pleasured. Once the footage was obtained, the camera shifted focus, tracking downward, cutting the woodsman's head out of the shot, and the day's indisputably one true thing landed on the heaving, freckled, fake breasts of the porn star kneeling at his feet.

Someone applauded. The scene broke. The female stars retreated to their trailers. The crew milled around the craft service table, picking at a platter of raw vegetables coupled with ranch dip and a large bowl of Fritos.

I sat down in a folding chair in the shade. Apparently, a supposed $250,000 budget bought you a plot as

substantive as tissue paper and an orgy atop a fire vehicle. Behind the scenes, it was less like watching people
have sex and more like witnessing an Olympic event in
which people copulated for sport. The sex was almost
incidental.

"Whaddya think?" One of the woodsmen who had
been pretending to be a fireman was standing over me, his
legs straddling mine. A dark-haired, olive-skinned former
nurse named Mickey G., he was married to yet another
blond porn star, the sweet, soft-spoken Missy. Shirtless,
he was still wearing his yellow fireman pants and red sus-
penders, caught between roles. He was the one who got the
blow job up the ladder. Now his groin was a foot from my
face. I looked up at him, shielding the sun with my hand,
wondering if he was trying to make a point, and what that
point was.

"Well, it certainly is interesting!" I said. And it *was*. The
experience was surreal. I had stepped into an otherworld
in which the old rules no longer applied, where people
screwed in public lots atop fire trucks and ejaculating on
command was part of the job description.

For all of porn's ridiculous aspects, and those are legion,
it was deeply revelatory to witness its making. Beyond the
smoke and mirrors—the fake orgasms, the unreal bodies,
the cockamamie premises—there was something more. In
porn, humanity was laid bare.

By the following January I had gotten my things
together and moved to LA. I rented a sunny, one-bedroom
apartment in Los Feliz, a hip east-side neighborhood. I
would spend the next several years working as a freelance

journalist. Sex was my stated focus, but my true interests lay in the Valley.

On a regular basis, I would drive over the Cahuenga Pass, where, in the late nineteenth century, California state senator Charles Maclay had stood on a hill and purportedly proclaimed of the pastoral valley landscape on the other side of the mountain range that separated the San Fernando Valley from LA proper: "This is the Garden of Eden!" I landed a job with Playboy TV as an on-camera reporter for a show titled *Sexcetera*, in which I and five or so other reporters traveled the world covering sex-related news stories, a program one of its producers referred to as "*60 Minutes* on Viagra." Each segment was approximately eight minutes long because that's how long it would take for the average guy to masturbate to it. When people asked me what I did on the show, I explained, "I talk to the camera while people have sex behind me." I went to the Playboy Mansion three times, where I met Hugh Hefner, hung out in its infamous grotto, and watched flamingos pick their way across the lawn as monkeys in outdoor cages hooted at the assembled guests. I went to a fetish party in London. I visited a strip club in Paris. I interviewed porn stars, prostitutes, pornographers, strippers, and gigolos. In a Canoga Park soundstage, I witnessed over a hundred men have sex with one woman on a human-size Lazy Susan, and at one point two men high-fived each other while double-teaming her. In a North Hollywood building with a brick façade and a sign that read BUILDING, I beheld in the neighborhood of eighty men ejaculate onto the face of a woman wearing a plastic collar fastened around her neck with duct tape. In a house on the property of a Van Nuys junkyard, I watched a male porn star dressed as a zombie copulate with a woman dressed like a schoolgirl.

At my apartment, I amassed a large collection of porn movies, more than any guy I knew had. Several times a week, I would hear the UPS driver bounding up the stairs to deposit a cardboard box of VHS videotapes on my doorstep. After a while, I ran out of space to store the videos, and they ended up piled on the floors of my closets, stacked in my built-in cabinets, tucked under my bed. I received a free subscription to *Adult Video News*, the porn industry's trade magazine, which featured the hottest adult stars on its covers, listed the bestselling X-rated titles, and ran a slavering column called "Fresh off the Bus," which profiled the newest starlets to have joined the ranks of those who had come to Los Angeles to be actresses, but for whatever reason—they were too short, or too lacking in ambition, or not good enough actors—had come to the Valley, from somewhere else, like Topeka, Kansas, or Laredo, Texas, or Kenosha, Wisconsin, to be a star in the porn business, so a star, nevertheless.

On the set of a porn movie, when the girl was in the middle, and the black eye of the camera was bearing down upon her, and the men had formed a half circle around her, I felt more alive than I did anywhere else. I had no explanation for this, did not report this to anyone, neglected to inform my boyfriend at the time of this.

And after I left the scene, as I came around the far east end of the Valley, past a stretch of the Los Angeles River known as the Narrows, where the indigenous Tongva had long ago lived in small villages, I experienced a kind of numbing, a sort of deadening, as if returning to the real world was a letdown, and Pornland was the place where I could be myself. Eventually, my brain would adjust, and I would return to reality. It was a kind of disassociating, but I didn't realize that until later.

A year or so after I moved to LA, I got a letter from Jack. Our last assessment in the Block Project, at age thirty-two, was on the horizon. Would I be willing to participate? We would not be returning to Tolman Hall. (That was too complex; over the last three decades they had surveyed us, our lives would have taken us around the globe, in some cases.) As I had every other time, I responded yes. A thick questionnaire arrived in the mail. There were so many questions. Was I in a relationship, married, or divorced? Were my parents alive or dead? Was I straight, gay, bisexual, or other? Was I happy and fulfilled or unhappy and restless? Did I have a lot of friends or was I more of a loner? Had my life turned out as I had expected or had it veered off course into unexpected waters? As I wrote my answers, I did my best to be truthful, but my responses had a positive spin, as if I were a child seeking to impress a parent I had seen infrequently and not in a long time.

A few days later, I yanked open the door on the mailbox down the street and tossed in the envelope. It struck me that the examiners, with their close study, active listening, and studious note taking, had taught me how to be a journalist. Maybe there was something about being in the study that had drawn me to write about the sex business. It seemed to me that the porn stars, strippers, and escorts that I was writing about and I had something in common: that need to be seen, that desire to be exceptional, to feel, above all else, *special.* I *got* it, I thought.

Over the years that followed in LA, I appeared on TV more than a hundred times. I published over a hundred articles, essays, and columns in magazines, newspapers, and weeklies, and on websites. I created one of the first sex blogs, *The Reverse Cowgirl*, which was widely read. At a Playboy convention, I autographed Polaroid photos of myself for *Sexcetera* fans. I established myself as something of an expert in the field of human sexuality.

But after five and a half years, I was burned out, my brain tired, my heart broken after my boyfriend broke up with me. In grad school, I'd written fiction. Maybe I would go somewhere and write a novel set in the porn business. On my computer, I surveyed a map of the United States. *I've never been to the South. New Orleans sounds cool. Bourbon Street, 24/7, 365-days-a-year bacchanalia. Mardi Gras beads and Spanish moss.*

On a hazy August morning, I tossed my porn videos and the silicone vagina molded to resemble a porn star's that someone had given me in trash bags and dropped them by the curb for the garbage truck.

The next day, I left LA.

Two years later, I peered at my computer screen, where the eye of Hurricane Katrina was churning toward Louisiana. The last couple of years hadn't turned out as I'd hoped. The novel had been slow going, and I had been freelance writing but not making a lot of money. I had published a short-story collection with an independent press, and that had sold six hundred copies.

Soon the Category 5 storm would make landfall. This would be no ordinary storm. It was growing to four hundred miles across with maximum sustained winds of 175 miles an hour. My hand shook as I clicked through pages of predictions of where the direct hit would be.

I got up and moved through the pink shotgun-style house I had rented a few blocks from the Mississippi River on a street named for a saint who was skinned alive. I had to get out of New Orleans—but how? My homicide detective boyfriend had turned into my ex-boyfriend a few months before, and there was no way I was going to beg him to come and rescue me. I had sold my car when I moved here from LA. What the fuck was I going to do? Out-pedal the hurricane on the pink bicycle I used to get around town? I would take a bus: anywhere. I grabbed the phone and called a taxi.

"The bus station's closed." The cabdriver turned the wheel, following the direction of the policeman shooing him away from the entrance.

"Shit." I tried not to hyperventilate.

"Where to?"

"Home, back home." I was stuck.

I paid the cabdriver. From my front porch I scanned

the sky. It was an eerie shade of orange. The couple that lived in the other half of the house was out of town. No, wait. She was gone, but he wasn't. Inside, I called my neighbor. She promised he would pick me up before he evacuated. I wasn't out of the woods, not yet, not by a long shot, but I had a ride, at least.

Eight hours later, I was in a car, heading northwest for Baton Rouge. Night had fallen. The traffic in front of us inched forward at a snail's pace. The lanes going in the opposite direction, to New Orleans, were deserted. A drop of rain hit the windshield. Then another. Then too many to count. It was the outer rainbands. The monster storm was upon us.

Usually, it would take an hour and a half to get to Baton Rouge from New Orleans. As the population of lower Louisiana fled, it took us eleven. In Baton Rouge, we stayed the night in a stranger's house with a dozen other refugees, sleeping on chairs and sofas and the floor. That Tuesday, we watched the news. The levees broke. The Crescent City flooded.

"Did Mom call?" I was walking on a road near the house in Baton Rouge a few days later, talking to my sister on my mobile phone. Ever since I had moved to LA, my relationship with my mother had been more and more distant. Since I'd moved to New Orleans, I'd heard from her less and less. Sometimes I would call her up and tell her about my life, what I was writing or who I was dating or my thoughts on some book or the other I was reading that maybe she had read too, but she would fall silent. She seemed bored, uninterested, like she wanted to be somewhere else doing something else. It hurt, but she was my mother, so I kept trying. Still, it felt like I was running my head into a brick wall, hoping my head would break through it.

"No." My sister hadn't heard from my mother. "Did she call you?"

"I haven't heard from her." I covered my eyes with my free hand. In all likelihood, my mother was sitting in the smaller Berkeley house she had bought after she had sold the house in which we had grown up. She could not have missed the news, which was broadcasting Hurricane Katrina coverage all day, every day. There were people on rooftops screaming to be rescued. There were dead bodies floating in the water. Had she not been curious to find out if I had survived? She had not. I thought of her saying, *I don't want to be a mother anymore.*

Since I couldn't return to New Orleans, I bought a plane ticket and flew to Virginia to stay with my best friend from grad school, Lydia. In her attic bedroom, I squeezed myself into her son's red racecar bed. I felt bad I had still not heard from my mother, stupid for being an adult whose life was a disaster, and relieved Lydia's family had taken me in.

In Louisiana, the National Guard had cordoned off the neighborhood in which I had been living, so it took some time before I could return to see what was left. That November, in a rented car, I drove through the broken city, and I wept, because it was so sad, how beautiful the city had been and how ruined it had been by what had transpired. The waters had receded. Refrigerators stood on the sidewalks like tombstones. Houses were in ruins.

I pulled up in front of the shotgun house. A sign on the front door stated that the roof shingles were made with asbestos so I should not enter. I opened the door and stepped inside. In the front room, I looked up through the ceiling slats and could see the blue sky; it was as if a giant had arrived in my absence and peeled back the roof like a lid on a tin can to get at what it wanted inside. All the videotapes of my TV appearances and clippings of articles I had written were trashed. Intricate black mold decorated the walls like lace. A pile of drywall covered my bed. In the backyard a hundred-year-old pecan tree had been uprooted and tossed aside like a toothpick. I picked out my belongings that had not been wrecked, including a box of papers that contained the letters I had gotten from the Block Project, and both my father's cremains and the cremains of my cat Kurtis, who had passed away before I had moved away from LA, and loaded them in the rental car. I drove past a boat on a sidewalk, and across a half-collapsed bridge over Lake Pontchartrain, and through miles of ravaged forest.

In Virginia, I decided it would be best for me to stay near Lydia for a while. I rented an apartment. I couldn't think straight, so I got a job as waitress in a restaurant. I had escaped the storm, but in my mind the troubled waters had closed over my head.

FOUR

Over the next several years, I struggled with post-traumatic stress disorder. I had escaped the storm's wrath, but the experience had short-circuited my brain. In Virginia, my thoughts were disconnected, scrambled, disarrayed. I had anxiety attacks, a recurring nightmare in which I was drowning, an emotional deadening. I did not feel like myself, but as if the self I had been was surgically removed, leaving behind a simulacrum of myself to inhabit the same body.

Sometimes on busy weekend nights in the upscale Italian restaurant where I worked as a waitress, as I and the other black-clad, apron-wearing, supplicating servers scrambled to meet the gastrological demands of wealthy diners in coats and ties and nice dresses—who arrived in BMWs, Mercedes-Benzes, and the occasional Ferrari, who avoided looking us in the eye so as not to be forced to recognize as fellow humans the people who were waiting on them, who left overpriced plates of chicken Parmesan and osso buco and penne alla vodka half eaten and ordered $100 bottles of wine without thinking twice—my mind would drift to my old life in Los Angeles, and it would seem like a life that had happened to someone else.

But something kept pushing me forward. I earned enough money waitressing to pay the bills. On the side, I wrote freelance articles. I reported a story for the local newspaper about an army veteran who had driven a Humvee over an IED in Iraq and had been burned over 34 percent of his body. I resurrected my blog. I signed up for a dating website and went on a few dates. My cracked brain began healing. In 2008, three years after I landed in Virginia, I was hired as an editor for a website that catered to the varied interests of eighteen-to-thirty-four-year-old women, called The Frisky, where I oversaw a stable of contributing writers and wrote about celebrities, fashion, and sex, and I quit waitressing.

By the spring of 2010, I was ready to try someplace new. As a freelancer, I could live anywhere. I considered moving back to LA, but it was too expensive. I had heard Austin, Texas—its motto: "Keep Austin Weird"—was affordable. I decided to move there. I was sad to leave my best friend but ready to leave the nest. In Austin, I rented a loft downtown. I kept freelancing, got paid to blog, and started writing ad copy for brands. I went on a few more dates. A year later, I decided to move to Chicago, where I had lived during grad school and where an ad agency for which I worked was based.

On the plane, I read Paul Auster's *City of Glass*. In it,

there's a Baudelaire quote: "*Il me semble que je serais toujours bien là où je ne suis pas.*" This line is translated as: "It seems to me that I will always be happy in the place where I am not." I looked out the window, at whatever part of the country we were flying over. I was that quote or that quote was me. I was searching for happiness or love or a place that felt like home. After my father had died, I had become estranged from my stepmother. After the hurricane, I had become estranged from my mother. After that, my sister and I had had a falling-out, and I had become estranged from her too. It was just me. Maybe Chicago would be the place where I would find what I was looking for.

On the North Side, I rented an apartment in a brown brick building. On a dating app, I met a television news producer. He was Irish, smart, funny. He also drank a lot and was gone a lot, jetting off to far-flung locations on dangerous assignments, covering the war in Afghanistan or the Egyptian revolution. We started talking about moving in together.

That fall, on a Friday night, we met for dinner at an Italian restaurant. As I inserted another forkful of pesto linguine into my mouth, I realized he was dumping me.

"You want something I can't give you," he said. "Wouldn't you *agree?*" I surveyed his bloodshot green eyes, ruddy skin, days-old stubble. What did he think I wanted that he thought he couldn't give me? Suddenly *I* wasn't sure what I wanted. Did *he* know what I wanted? I thought about asking him what he thought I wanted. Then I thought better of it.

"You have no idea what I want," I declared defensively.

Never get married! My mother had started saying that after my father had left her. *A woman needs a man like a fish needs a bicycle!* she would exhort, quoting her favorite feminist. *Gloria Steinem never got married,* she would add. *And you shouldn't either.* (When Steinem got married, in 2000, my mother stopped saying this.) Since my parents' divorce, my mother had had only one serious relationship, a decade-long affair with a married professor. Following her directive, I had remained single, like Carrie Bradshaw on *Sex and the City.* And what did I have to show for it? Yet another failed relationship.

"Can I give you a ride home?" he offered on the sidewalk in front of the restaurant. I shivered in the chilly night air. A deep freeze was coming.

Without answering, I stomped off, pulling my black wool winter coat tighter around me. The autumn leaves crunched under the high heels of my black boots. I vowed never to be made to feel this way again. Next time, *I* would be the one doing the dumping, dammit.

Back at my apartment, I unlocked the door and flipped on the light switch. I went to the steam radiator and cranked the stiff knob; the radiator came to life, hissing like a snake. I hung up my coat and plopped onto my bed to pull off my boots. I lay back on the mattress. What if I was destined to end up like my mother, unhappy and alone…forever?

I knew what I had to do. I flipped over and pulled out my laptop. I typed the URL of a dating website into my browser. I dashed off a profile and uploaded a few photos: a sultry mirror selfie, drunkish at a bar with friends in New

York City, posing saucily in a black dress and high heels at a New Year's Eve party. Who was I looking for? the form wanted to know. A guy who was *never, ever boring*, I asserted, chuckling to myself. I began scanning the sea of faces. Right away, one caught my eye. He had dark eyes and dark hair (my type), and he was tall (six-three), like me (I'm six-one). He was a corporate executive and a lieutenant colonel in the United States Marine Corps Reserve, who, I would learn, had deployed to Iraq twice, as part of Operation Iraqi Freedom. I studied a smiling photo of him. He had a giant yellow boa constrictor draped across his shoulders. He didn't seem boring. I sent him a digital wink and closed my laptop.

The next morning, there was a message from the boa constrictor guy waiting for me. We exchanged a few flirty messages. We arranged to meet for drinks.

A week later, I scanned the crowded bar.

He's handsome, I thought, when I spotted him. I made my way over. We shook hands. The bar was packed, so we headed up the street to a nearby restaurant.

"I Googled you," he stated as he tucked into his steak.

I stared at my salmon. If he had searched my name, he had learned I wrote about sex. Of course, sex wasn't the only thing I wrote about. I wrote about other things, too: movies, TV shows, art, fashion, breaking news, politics, books, food, travel. Even so, the sex stuff was the only thing guys ever remembered after Googling me.

"I'm *intrigued*." He grinned. He raised his fork and started reciting my Wikipedia page. "I have a photographic memory." His IQ was 150-something, he shared.

After dinner, I let him drive me home. In front of my building, I remained in the passenger seat. He didn't try to kiss me. I walked up my front path. Maybe he wasn't interested.

The next day, he asked me out again. That Friday, he picked me up and took me on a whirlwind date that spanned the city: lunch in Chinatown, a walk along the lakefront, wine and cheese at a hip Wicker Park wine bar. At dusk, we went to his town house in Evanston, a suburb north of Chicago, where I met his Chesapeake Bay retrievers: Jake, a male, and Coco, a female. That night, we had sex. I didn't leave until Monday morning.

On Tuesday, I was perched on a stool at his kitchen counter. He was stirring a boiling pot of spaghetti. As I watched him, I felt myself falling for him, losing my balance.

"I had this *idea*," he said with a conspiratorial wink. "What do you say we fly to Las Vegas this weekend and—" He paused dramatically. "Get married?"

"Are you kidding me?"

Quickly, I did the math. I had never been married; he had been married once. Neither of us had kids. We weren't getting any younger. *Why wait?* I figured. I slid off the stool, walked around the counter, and wrapped my arms around his neck.

"Yes," I said with a laugh.

Nine days after our first date, we exchanged generic wedding vows in the same little brown wood chapel on the south end of the Vegas Strip where Angelina Jolie had married Billy Bob Thornton. I wore a cream-colored one-shoulder ruched cocktail dress and gold stilettos I had bought at Nordstrom, and he wore a brown suit from his closet. No one we knew was present.

And just like that, I was married.

That night, I lay naked in bed next to my sleeping husband in the king-size bed of the upper-floor luxury hotel room on the Vegas Strip in which we were staying. My dress was on the floor. On the table near the window, the remaining chocolate-covered strawberries sat on a plate next to the drained bottle of Veuve Clicquot champagne. My bouquet of cream-colored roses, baby's breath, and fern fronds was in an ice bucket filled with water. I stared at the ceiling, unable to sleep from all the excitement. It had happened so fast. I was *a wife.*

I had found my Prince Charming, but I had kissed a lot of frogs along the way. I had lost track of my number— the number of guys I'd had sex with, that is. Thirty-five, at least. Closer to thirty-eight, probably. Forty or more, likely. There was K., whose younger brother I went to high school with and who devirginized me in the guesthouse in which he stayed behind his parents' house. There was N., my first boyfriend, whom I met at community college, and who stole my debit card and used it to withdraw money from my account and then lied to me about it when I confronted him (had I really given him my PIN?). There was T., the real estate agent I encountered at a San Francisco nightclub, whom I had sex with that night and never again.

There was B., an offensive lineman for an NFL team, whom I dated for a few months when I was a grad student, and who, at six-foot-six and three hundred pounds, made me feel petite by comparison. There was R., a moody LA artist who built flame-shooting robots and who let me fire his flamethrower on our first date, sealing the deal. There was A., the famous comedian, who kept four sex dolls in various rooms of his Hollywood Hills house, the silicone tongue of one of which came off in my hand when I tugged at it while he was in the kitchen getting us beer. There was G., the homicide detective I dated for a year when I lived in New Orleans, who looked like Elvis and whom I fell madly in love with but who ended our relationship for reasons that were unclear. There were others, too, men whose names, faces, and body types were lost to time. Looking back, it seemed like I had spent decades wandering in a forest of penises. In the end, all that fondling, blowing, and penetrating led me to where I was.

I snagged my digital camera from the nightstand. I had used it to take photos throughout the day. I stopped on the one in the hotel room's bathroom mirror before we left for the chapel. My hair was a dead straight bob, thanks to a stylist. The sculptural pouf on my one-shoulder dress added a dramatic flourish. But the camera obscured my face.

I put the camera back and curved myself around my husband. I was the big spoon. He was the little spoon. I could feel the heat radiating off him, the steady rise and fall of his breath, the reliable metronome of his heart. Far below, people were walking up and down the Strip, searching for money, sex, drugs, excitement, a version of themselves they wished to be and were unlikely to become. Up here, I was safe, protected, enwombed. This was the thing for which I had been searching.

Four days later, on a crisp late November morning, I boarded an elevated train that took me to a downtown hospital where I had an appointment for my annual mammogram. At the hospital, I rode the elevator to the fourth floor. From the waiting room, I was escorted to a dressing room. I swapped my black turtleneck for a voluminous pink smock that tied in the front. I took a seat in a chair alongside the other women in pink smocks waiting to have their mammograms.

A woman called my name. I followed her down the hall. In the examination room, I opened my gown, stood close to the machine, and embraced it awkwardly. She lifted my right breast onto the cool surface. A translucent plate lowered. The tissue compressed. I winced. She went to stand at the monitor.

"Hold your breath."

The machine hummed. She moved back and forth between the machine and the monitor, positioning and repositioning me, checking and rechecking the images. The same routine followed with my left breast.

"I'm going to check with the doctor."

I sat in a chair to wait.

When she returned, she said the doctor had requested

a few more scans. *There's nothing wrong,* I told myself as she scanned and rescanned my right breast. *You're a newlywed. You still need to go on your honeymoon.*

"Wait here," she said.

Ten minutes later, she reappeared. She led me to a cramped office. I took a seat. I surveyed the shelves. They were filled with medical books bearing incomprehensible titles.

This isn't good, I thought.

The door opened. A pretty, small-boned, serious doctor in a white coat and a wide-faced, heavyset, short-haired woman—a nurse?—entered the room.

This isn't good at all.

"I can't deal with this," I said and burst into tears.

The nurse secured me by the wrists.

"Just listen to what she has to say," she advised.

"See, right there." The doctor pointed to the image of my right breast on the wall-mounted digital screen. Amid the fine, delicate lines, there was a cloudy spot. It looked like a ghost, as if my breast were haunted. "Those are calcifications. There are three kinds of calcifications: the good kind, the bad kind, and the we-don't-know kind. You have the we-don't-know kind. You'll have to come back. We need to do a biopsy."

In the dressing room, I pulled my turtleneck over my head. Surely, this was much ado about nothing. Without a doubt, the doctor was prescribing more tests than were necessary out of an abundance of caution. Until now I had paid little attention to my breasts, which were relatively small—a B-cup. I had done nothing that would make them want to murder me. My tits were fine. My boobs were not deadly. My breasts were benign.

"It's nothing to worry about, right?" I asked my husband that night. (After we got married, I moved in with him, although some of my stuff was still at my apartment.) He had survived a *war* on the other side of the world. Even if things were to get bad, he would know what to do. Wouldn't he?

"You have nothing to worry about." He wrapped me in a bear hug.

A couple of weeks later, I was prone on a metal table, my right breast hanging through a hole in the bed upon which I was lying, undergoing a core needle biopsy. A metal plate was smashing my breast so it wouldn't move. At the monitor, the doctor guided the needle, extracting bite-size pieces of flesh.

Afterward, the nurse bandaged my breast so it wouldn't bleed all over me. At the doorway, I stopped to examine the petri dish that contained what the doctor had harvested. The tissue resembled cooked baby shrimps.

On Saturday, my husband and I were at Costco, idling in the pet food aisle, when my mobile phone rang. The number was from the hospital.

"You have breast cancer," a man's voice related. I sat down hard on a forty-pound bag of dog food and handed the phone to my husband. As I would learn, it was early-stage, but it wasn't a garden-variety type of breast cancer, the kind of breast cancer I might have chosen had I been given the opportunity to pick one in the breast cancer aisle of a supermarket that sold Things That Might

Kill Me. The kind of breast cancer I had was A Very Bad Kind. It would furrow the brows of the many doctors I would encounter on what is sometimes referred to as a *cancer journey*.

"We'll have to do a double mastectomy." In the examination room, the terse, business-like, expressionless oncologist studied me, seeking to gauge my reaction, her eyes large behind her thick glasses. "We should talk about doing a hysterectomy, too. But let's not get ahead of ourselves on that. I'm going to bring in someone you should talk to for your post-double-mastectomy breast reconstruction. He's a plastic surgeon."

"What happens if I get a double mastectomy?" I asked the physician's assistant as we waited for the oncologist to return with the plastic surgeon.

"You know, I probably shouldn't say this." He held up his left hand, his palm flat and facing upward. "This is the wall of your chest." He formed his right hand into a tent shape. "This is your breast tissue." He placed the tented hand on top of the flat hand. "This is what happens when you get a mastectomy." The tented hand collapsed onto the flat hand. "It's like a circus tent without the pole."

The plastic surgeon appeared, clutching a photo album. The photos in it featured headless women, their scarred, mutilated breasts exposed for my review. He smiled reassuringly. The Frankenboobs terrified me. I slammed the photo album closed.

"That was awful," I told my husband as we drove home.

Shortly thereafter, we switched to a hospital in Highland Park, a suburb north of Chicago. A few months later, a highly recommended surgical oncologist performed the breast-conserving lumpectomy that I needed, not the double mastectomy the other oncologist had told me I needed. The surgeon cut around the circumference of my areola and peeled back my nipple like a porthole to pry the mass from its moorings.

This was just the first step. I would need to see another oncologist who would tell me if I needed chemotherapy to wipe out any cancerous cells that had been left behind and to prevent the breast cancer from recurring. "This oncologist is the one I recommend," my surgical oncologist said, handing me a business card when I returned for a follow-up visit a few weeks later. The oncologist had an unusual name that conjured up an image of a magical beast.

A week later, my husband and I sat across from the oncologist, a short, warm man whom I liked right away. A collection of geodes was strewn across his desk. A framed artwork made by a patient depicted him as a superhero flying through the air, his head nurse as his sidekick flying alongside him.

"I would recommend chemotherapy," he said.

This wasn't what I had hoped to hear. Once my hair started falling out, everyone would know something was wrong with me. I started crying.

"You got this," my husband said, squeezing my hand. As the oncologist began to recite the protocol, I glanced over to check my husband's expression. He was playing the role of tough guy. I worried he was thinking: *I married a lemon.*

I underwent a second surgery, during which my surgeon installed a port-a-cath, turning me into a cyborg.

Every week, I went to the hospital for a chemo infusion. In the second week, my immune system crashed. At the three-week mark, I watched as strands of my hair slipped down the shower drain. Soon enough, I was bald, as was my mons pubis, like a prepubescent teen's. My fingernails and toenails turned brown and fell from their beds, a side effect of my chemo drug. I developed sores in my mouth and around my anus. My stomach churned, its lining burned. My bones ached. I felt like I was dying, and I looked like it, too. I was no longer the person I had been. I had turned into someone else: A Sick Person.

On an overcast day in the spring of 2012, I sat in a blue vinyl armchair in a private room on the hospital's cancer ward. A square window framed a field of heartland grass waving in the breeze under a gray sky heavy with impending rain. On a television set mounted to the wall near the ceiling next to the door, Dr. Phil reminded someone that the best predictor of future behavior was relevant past behavior. An IV pole hung with two bags of liquid containing a toxic cocktail—a chemo drug made from the bark of the Pacific yew tree, a wildly expensive gene-targeting drug for my aggressive type of breast cancer, a whopping dose of Benadryl, steroids to manage the side effects of the drugs, and a saline solution—beeped methodically, pumping the liquid through a clear plastic tube that snaked across the floor and disappeared under my blue hospital gown. Earlier, the nurse, a middle-aged brunette with a warm smile and a sarcastic sense of humor, had affixed the tube's pushpin-shaped needle to the port-a-cath that had been surgically implanted below my left collarbone and through which drugs were now flowing into an artery that led directly to my heart, for maximum efficacy. The nurse had a horizontal scar across the base of her neck that made it appear as if someone had tried to slit her throat but was from the thyroid cancer she had survived years before.

As Dr. Phil offered his guest a free stay in rehab, I tried to remember what day it was. *Monday. Tuesday. Friday.* In recent weeks, a thick "chemo fog," the term used to describe the cognitive difficulties and memory loss caused by chemo, had settled on my brain, making it hard to think. Moving carefully so as not to unplug myself from the IV, I swiveled the chair around to ask my husband what day it was. The room was empty. He was on a work trip, I recalled. *Brazil. China. Russia.* I couldn't remember for how long. Dr. Phil's guest agreed to go to rehab. The audience burst into applause. *Maybe I'm not married. Maybe I'm hallucinating from all the drugs.* I held up my left hand. On my ring finger, there was a white-gold band with a round diamond in a trapezoidal setting that was my engagement ring and a platinum band embedded with diamonds that was my wedding ring. I hadn't lost my mind—not yet.

I leaned my head back against the chair. The gentle tug of the Benadryl kicking in felt like an octopus had wrapped its tentacles around my ankle and was dragging me below the surface. I surrendered, letting it take me, and drifted into the blackness.

I woke a little while later. The IV was still beeping. I needed to pee, but I didn't want to press the button that would summon the nurse, who could help me navigate to the bathroom down the hall, and bother her with my bodily functions as if I were a child. Other patients sulked in their rooms, barked at the nurses, complained about symptoms. Not me. I was the perfect patient; if having cancer were a competition, I was *winning*. I grimaced as I slipped my legs off the side. The colorful crocheted throw blanket an elderly woman (I assumed not a lot of elderly men were into crochet) who lived at a nearby rest home had made for unfortunate, cancer-having people like me slid to the floor. I stood, wobbled, stabilized.

I grabbed the IV pole and shuffled to the door. The hall was empty. I headed for the bathroom, dragging the IV pole behind me like a dog on a leash. I focused on the floor, hoping the no-slip socks would prevent me from falling on my ass. As a rule, I tried not to look in the other rooms, but when I reached the end of the hall, I couldn't help myself. Across the way, the door was ajar. An ancient woman was lying in her bed. Her eyes were shut; she was never awake. Her white hair was a cloud on the pillow. Her sticklike arms were drawn onto her bony chest. Her mouth gaped. For her, I gathered, this was not a rest stop on the freeway of life but the final destination. More than anything else, I did not want to be her.

I closed the bathroom door behind me and leaned on the sink, catching my breath. From the mirror a woman stared out at me. She had burned-out holes for eyes, sallow skin, a moonlike face. She pulled the orange fleece cap from her head, exposing her naked skull. No wonder people veered away from her. She was the specter of death.

I sat on the freezing toilet seat, feeling bad for my husband, who had thought he had married me but had ended up married to the crazy woman in the mirror. I had sensed him pulling away, withdrawing someplace inside himself that was inaccessible to me. *You're a dime,* he had said when he saw me in my wedding dress. (*You're a ten,* he had meant.) I closed my eyes, placed my elbows on my thighs, and put my face in my hands. We hadn't had sex since I started chemo. My post-surgery right breast was smaller than the left. The port protruded hideously from my chest. Chemo had kicked me into early menopause. My body was not a wonderland. It was a Superfund site.

I returned to the treatment room and dozed off again. A knock at the door snapped me out of my drug-induced nap. The door swung open. A man stepped into the room. This was the other oncologist, the not-my-oncologist. My oncologist was at a cancer conference, where, with my permission, he was presenting my cancer case and the treatment that he was betting on curing me to a roomful of other cancer doctors. The not-my-oncologist was younger and strode the chemo ward halls with a cocky, self-assured swagger. I did not like him.

"Ms. Breslin!" the not-my-oncologist exclaimed.

"Yes, that's me," I said, pulling the blanket up over me.

"I have a few of our medical residents with me today," he said. "I would *love* to share your case with them." He bowed slightly. After all the appointments and the tests and the probes, I had come to the conclusion that I was something more than one more cancer patient to these doctors. To the oncologists, I was a *fascinating* specimen.

"All right, I guess, sure, that's fine," I said, feeling cornered.

The residents filed into the room and formed a semi-circle around me. The not-my-oncologist, my chart in his hand, rattled off the details of my *cancer profile*, a term that made me think of a dating profile on an imaginary website for cancerous tumors that were searching for a host body. *Hi, I'm a newly available, totally malignant tumor. I'm ER/PR negative, HER2+++, and I'm looking for my perfect match: a woman who is willing to make space for me in her chest. Let's connect!*

There was something familiar about the way the residents were looking at me. It was like I was being studied again. The hospital room was the experiment room. The doctors were the examiners. I was their subject. After the Block Project had ended in 1999, I hadn't thought about it all that often. But on a February morning in 2010, when I was living in Virginia, I had been reading *The New York Times* online when a headline had caught my eye:

JACK BLOCK, WHO STUDIED YOUNG CHILDREN INTO ADULTHOOD, DIES AT 85

I was one of those young children, I had thought. Jack, the obituary had reported, had died from complications related to a spinal injury that he had suffered a decade prior.

The hospital room door closed. My visitors were gone.

On the TV, a weepy soap opera star was confessing to a young man that she was not his aunt but the long-lost mother that he had believed was dead. Surely, the Blocks hadn't predicted this scene: me, the hospital, the tumor that had been inside of me. But, I wondered, what *had* they foreseen for me?

By September, I had finished chemotherapy and was starting to feel better. The mental fog had begun to lift. Peach-fuzz-like hairs had sprouted across my skull. The bone pain caused by the chemo drug had receded. But I wasn't done yet. Another six months of IV infusions of the gene-targeting cancer drug and six weeks of radiation were ahead of me.

On a Monday morning, I entered the radiation center. Half a dozen people were waiting to get irradiated. In the dressing room, I put on an oversize blue smock. I came back out and took a seat. To pass the time, I tried to guess what type of cancers the other people had. The balding man in khakis had prostate cancer, I speculated. The sixty-something woman in a housedress had lung cancer, I theorized. The nun with the patch over her eye had brain cancer, I was pretty sure of it. In this waiting room, as had been the case in every other waiting room in which I had waited, I was the youngest patient, which wasn't a good thing.

"Suzanne…Broysline?"

I trailed the woman down the hall and into a room in

the middle of which was a large machine that resembled an enormous microscope. At the other end of the room, a digital wall glowed pleasantly, programmed to display a virtual garden—mature trees, blooming foliage, a tranquil pool. It was a bit of cancer theater designed to have a calming effect on the soon-to-be-radiated. I untied my smock and lay faceup on the machine's bed. The eye of the machine hovered over me. The technician disappeared. The machine came to life. Green laser beams formed crosshairs on my chest. The machine rotated around me, whirring, humming, and beeping. My radiating had commenced.

I closed my eyes and thought about how despite all the chunks of flesh that had been extracted from my body, despite the dozens of tests I had undergone, despite the doctors' many thoughtful examinations of my breasts, no one could tell me *why* the tumor had materialized in the first place. Maybe it was the birth control pills I had taken. Maybe it was the years I had smoked. Maybe it was stress. The robot that didn't do any of these things and was incapable of making poor life choices continued shooting its photon beams at my right tit.

"A tumor is a lot like a fetus," an acupuncturist I had visited in a cramped second-floor office a few weeks before my radiation session had told me. "They're both just clusters of fast-growing cells." She had stuck another needle in my abdomen to emphasize her point.

Instead of a baby, I mused, *I had a tumor baby.* I saw myself on the surgical table, my surgeon inserting her stainless-steel tongs in the gaping hole where my right nipple had been, extracting the malignant mass, and holding the tumor up to the surgical light. Its tiny arms and legs flailed helplessly. The slit in its otherwise feature-less face opened, letting loose a stream of blood. My surgeon dropped the tumor baby into a stainless-steel pan. It landed with a *plop!*

It was possible this entire series of events had been set in motion long ago, a rung in the helix of my DNA that had been made wrong on the production line and that, as a result, had inevitably failed, like a blender that stops working the day after its warranty expires. According to my oncologist, the type of breast cancer I had was most likely to return in the first two years. Should I make it to five years, he had told me, I would be in the clear.

My thoughts drifted to the Block Project. The Blocks couldn't have predicted I would develop breast cancer, but they had predicted who I would grow up to be. Surely, they had maintained files on the cohort, files that had contained our individual data. Those files had held the stories of our lives. It was possible there was a file in a cabinet in a dusty storage room in the bowels of the UC Berkeley campus with my name on it. All I had to do was find it.

I had been their research subject for years, but I didn't know much about them or what they had learned about us over the three decades of the study. If you studied a kid, *could* you predict who that kid would grow up to be? Had they correctly guessed the type of person *I* would grow up to be? And what had happened to the other kids who were in the study—the cohort—where were *they*? The journalist sector of my brain kicked into gear. This was a story, one I could write, that would be unlike anything I had written before, one in which I would be my own subject. As a subject in the study, my role was clear: I was the one answering *their* questions. This time the roles would be reversed: *I* would be the one asking the questions.

As I drove home, I sang along to Florence and the Machine's "Dog Days Are Over" on the radio. One day, this part of my life would be a thing of the past, like a bad dream, or a shitty time best forgotten. The rest of my hair would grow back, the scar around my nipple and the scar where the port-a-cath had been (the surgeon had removed it after I finished chemo) would fade, and my marriage would have survived the worst thing that would happen to it.

FIVE

Contained within every marriage is a lie. In order to sustain a marriage, one tells small lies or big ones, changes one's personality to suit the needs of the other, or constructs a façade behind which one hides who one really is. It happens slowly or quickly, almost immediately or a long time later, without acknowledgment or as something everyone is aware of but no one speaks of. At some point the marriage becomes a fiction. One has an affair but it was on a work trip so it doesn't really count, or one flirts with an old high school boyfriend on Facebook but that's not reality so it doesn't matter. One bites one's tongue, or one says things one doesn't mean. One acquires a cache of porn that is kept in a computer file labeled WORK or TAXES or STUFF and with which one develops a deeply personal, almost romantic relationship, or one thinks about a fireman who was seen at a grocery store while one is masturbating. Sometimes when one looks in the mirror, one sees one's own outline is blurring, one is becoming less distinct, and one has been transformed into a shadow of oneself. In time, the former self only resurfaces when one is digging through clothes that haven't been worn in years hanging in the back of a closet or when one is going through a box that holds photos from years past or when one runs into someone from a long time ago with whom one used to be close but who now feels like a stranger. One thinks the lie is what has or hasn't been told to the husband or wife, partner or significant other, the wagon to which one is hitched or the ball to which one is chained, but the person is the lie. One is no longer oneself.

In the beginning of our relationship, my husband had swept me off my feet, love-bombing me with attention, presenting me with gifts in blue boxes from Tiffany, telling me the only thing he didn't like about our relationship was that we hadn't met when we were younger. But three weeks after I was diagnosed with breast cancer and barely a month after we got married, he revealed another side of him, and things changed.

One night, we drove north to have dinner at the home of a friend of my husband's and the friend's wife. After dinner, my husband and his friend went in the backyard to drink bourbon. Because of the drinking and the lateness, we decided we would spend the night. For a while, I talked to the wife on the living room sofa. It was close to midnight when I went to bed in a guest room, climbing under the blue-and-green-plaid flannel comforter. In the early-morning hours, the door opened, waking me. My husband stood in the doorway, backlit by the light spilling in behind him. He stumbled into the room, stripped to his boxers, and clambered onto the bed. In the half-light, he climbed on top of me, looming over me, on all fours.

"I want to beat the fucking shit out of you," he said. His breath was thick with the smell of alcohol. I lay frozen underneath him. I was terrified as to what he might do next. "I want to beat the fucking shit out of you," he said again.

Then he rolled off. A few moments later, he started snoring.

The next morning, I woke up first. He was sleeping peacefully.

"Do you know what you said last night?" He had woken with a hangover and hadn't said anything about what happened.

"No, what?"

"You told me you wanted to beat the shit out of me."

"I didn't say that." He claimed to have no memory of it.

As we drove home, I looked out the window. He had been *drunk*, I told myself. That hadn't been *him*. I decided to write the disturbing incident off as a drunken lapse.

In fact, my Prince Charming was more like Dr. Jekyll and Mr. Hyde. Sometimes I felt like he was considerate and thoughtful. Sometimes I felt like he was controlling and possessive. Every morning, he took a commuter train to work, his briefcase at his side. In his home office, a trio of framed college degrees hung on the wall. If he saw someone on the side of the road with a flat tire, he would fix it. He also had a hair-trigger temper and what I felt was a pathological desire to be seen as a tough guy. A Saturday morning drive to Costco in which we encountered too much traffic pushed him to the brink of road rage. He obsessed over bills he didn't think were fair. He was intense, intimidating, and sometimes he frightened me.

As a journalist, I had dealt with plenty of so-called alpha males. The sex business was full of them. Clad in the armor of toxic masculinity, these men masked their insecurities and manipulated other people to feel a sense of control. Not only had I known my husband was a tough guy when I had met him, it was part of *why* I had married him. He had made me feel safe, like I was protected. Besides, I'd assumed, it wasn't like he was going to do anything bad to *me*.

During my breast cancer treatment, he'd suggested I stop working, so I had scaled back on freelancing. He preferred it when *he* was my sole focus. Feeling guilty for having derailed our marriage with my breast cancer diagnosis, I tried to give him what I thought he wanted. I did the laundry, made dinner, and got on my knees to scrub the splatter of his fecal matter off the toilet bowl until the porcelain sparkled. To make him happy, I gave up a part of myself.

"Florida?"

"Florida."

He had come home from work with the news. Another company wanted to hire him. The new position was based in Southwest Florida. The money was great. It would be a promotion, a step up the ladder for him.

"I've never been to Florida," I told him.

"I used to spend summers there with my grandparents,"

he said. "The beaches are incredible. The weather is amazing. Not like it is here."

I looked out the window above the sink. I had finished my breast cancer treatment in the spring. Now snowflakes were drifting past the glass. In the morning, he would have to shovel a path from the front door and through the alley so he could get out the car. Tomorrow, it was expected to be in the low teens. I was from California. To me living in Illinois was like living in Siberia. Besides, Florida could be a chance for us to start over.

It was April when the movers took our furniture and boxes. We packed the rest in the car and drove south. In the back seat, Coco panted in her bed, her toys strewn around her. (We had put down Jake, who was terminally ill.) The flat fields of the Midwest turned into the sloping hills of the South. Two days later, we crossed the border between Georgia and Florida. I eyeballed the WELCOME TO FLORIDA sign.

"You know what Florida's nickname is?" my husband asked, smiling as we barreled down the interstate. " 'God's waiting room.' People come here to die."

In Southwest Florida, we lived in a sleepy coastal town where hurricanes seldom made landfall, multi-million-dollar mansions overlooked pristine white sand beaches and the tranquil aqua waters of the Gulf of Mexico, and retirees from points north passed their days playing golf and pickleball. For several months, we stayed in a two-bedroom apartment my husband's employer had rented for us. A few days before Christmas, we moved into the first home I had ever owned, a yellow Mediterranean-style house on the curving main road of a gated and planned community. It had a perfectly manicured lawn of St. Augustine grass, a backyard swimming pool, and a view of a man-made lake.

"I'll see you tonight," I told my husband and kissed him goodbye. From the porch, I watched as his car went around the corner. I surveyed the street. No cars drove down it. No people walked on the sidewalks. All the houses looked the same. It reminded me of *The Truman Show*, the 1998 movie starring Jim Carrey as Truman Burbank, whose every living moment since his conception has been broadcast to the entire world from a set on a soundstage and who has no idea that everyone he knows is an actor, including his wife.

In the primary bedroom, I peeled off my peach T-shirt and gray nylon running shorts. In my walk-in closet, I grabbed my black bikini and put it on. From the bedroom, I padded barefoot across the travertine floor, past the kitchen and the living room. At the far end of the main living area, I opened a sliding glass door that led to the pool. I closed it behind me so Coco couldn't escape. I tossed my towel on a chair and climbed down the pool ladder, slipping into the water. I dog-paddled to the deep end. I dove downward. From the bottom of the pool, I looked upward. Sunbeams pierced the surface, streaming through the water. I wondered what would happen if I were to open my mouth and inhale the water. My lungs would feel like they were going to explode. Everything would go black. My body would float to the top for my husband to find when he got home from work tonight. I pushed myself off the bottom, burst through the surface, gasped for air.

I pulled myself out of the pool and flopped onto the patio, still heaving. I had everything I'd thought I wanted, but I wasn't *happy*. I had ended up in an alternate reality, living someone else's life. My career had stalled. I hadn't written anything of any consequence in what seemed like forever. I had bent over backward to make my husband happy, and I had wound up in *Florida*, of all places, where I knew no one, for the sake of his career. I was a bit player in his life story. *Is this all there is?* I started to blubber. *Is this the story of my life?*

As I lay there, it occurred to me that if I was responsible for having gotten myself into this situation, I was the one who was responsible for getting myself out of it. I sat up and wiped the snot from my nose. I dried my eyes with the towel, smearing mascara across my face. I peeled off my wet bikini, not caring if the neighbors saw. I walked nude into the house. In the bedroom, I put on a dry shirt, underpants, and shorts. Now was the time, dammit.

It was time to write my own story. In the front bedroom, which I had claimed as my home office, I sat down at my desk. I opened Google's search page on my computer. I typed two words into the search bar: *Block Project*. I clicked the SEARCH button.

Thousands of results unscrolled on the page. There were published papers—"Nursery School Personality and Political Orientation Two Decades Later," "The Personality of Children Prior to Divorce: A Prospective Study," "Adolescent Drug Use and Psychological Health. A Longitudinal

Inquiry"—numerous articles—"Early Childhood May Offer Clues of Future Drug Use," "The Kids Are OK: Divorce and Children's Behavior Problems," "Were Conservatives Whiny Children?"—multiple obituaries—"Jack Block, Leader in Human Development, Dies," "Jeanne H. Block Dies; Research Psychologist," "Jack Block, 85; Psychologist Studied Children over Time"—various Wikipedia biographies, for Jack: "His most renowned body of work, undertaken primarily with his wife, was a longitudinal study on a cohort of more than 100 San Francisco Bay Area toddlers"; for Jeanne: "She conducted research into sex-role socialization and, with her husband Jack Block, created a person-centered personality framework"; and the Child Study Center: "one of the oldest continuously running centers for the study of children in the country"; and photos: of Jack, of Jeanne, of the preschool.

Had I never known the real name of the study or had I forgotten it? I Googled *Block and Block Longitudinal Study, 1969–1999.* That search produced a link to the Henry A. Murray Research Archive, an "endowed repository for quantitative and qualitative research data at the Institute for Quantitative Social Science," at Harvard University. The Murray Archive had materials related to the Block Project. The files had been digitized and uploaded to its password-protected website. I navigated to the page where our study's files were. I clicked a file. Nothing happened. I noticed a small digital burgundy padlock. It was locked.

Murray, I learned, had been a prominent Harvard psychologist and the director of the Harvard Psychological Clinic who had been interested in personality. During

World War II, he had left Harvard and was a lieutenant colonel for the Office of Strategic Services, the predecessor of the Central Intelligence Agency. During his service with the OSS, he had helped develop a personality profile of Adolf Hitler; the report had predicted the leader of the Nazi Party would commit suicide rather than surrender to the enemy and suggested Hitler was impotent and possibly gay. After his stint with the OSS, Murray had returned to Harvard. There he had launched a three-year study of twenty-two male Harvard undergraduates, the youngest of whom was a seventeen-year-old Theodore John Kaczynski, who would become the Unabomber. The students had been subjected to extreme stress tests; the sessions, Murray would confess years after, were "vehement, sweeping and personally abusive." One article speculated Murray's study had been part of the CIA's infamous Project MKUltra, a "mind control" program that had involved experiments on humans, including the dosing of some of the CIA's own unsuspecting agents, prisoners, mental patients, prostitutes, and drug addicts with lysergic acid diethylamide—or LSD. Had Kaczynski's tenure as a human lab rat turned him into a builder of bombs that had killed three people and injured more than twenty others, or had there been something inside of him all along that had destined him to be that way?

I checked the time. Three hours had passed. With a few clicks, I had been transported to a strange new world where researchers were gods, students were guinea pigs, and the pursuit of scientific inquiry was more important than its subjects' humanity.

There was a term for what I had been part of: *human subject research*. The Block Project and its role in my psychological development had been something about which I had thought little and spent even less time psychoanalyzing. That was about to change.

That night, my husband turned off the light and slipped into our king-size bed. He edged closer to me and threw his arm across my torso. This was his idea of foreplay. He climbed on top of me, inserting himself inside of me. He slung my calves over his shoulders, pressed my thighs down with his hands, and began thrusting robotically in and out. Pinned down, I could barely move. That was the point, it seemed. For him my desirable state was immobile.

Afterward, I watched the ceiling fan spin in lazy circles as my husband snored beside me. In the brief window of time between when we had met and when we had married, we had talked about kids; having them, that is. Since we were older, we agreed we would adopt, preferably an older kid. But then I had been diagnosed with breast cancer. No, scratch that. Then I had gotten pregnant with the tumor baby. Before I had met my husband, I had had unsafe sex more times than I could count with more sex partners than I could recall with any accuracy, but I had never gotten pregnant, not even once. A gynecologist had remarked, her head between my legs with my feet in the stirrups, some unseen stainless-steel medical instrument plunged inside of me: *Your cervix is incredibly tight!* Womb-wise, I was a gated fortress, impenetrable, and impregnable. The tumor baby had found another way in.

On that freezing February day three years earlier, the surgeon had disposed of the tumor baby as if it had been one more glob of human tissue to be destroyed, along with the amputated limbs, liposuctioned fat, and diseased organs that went into the hospital trash. I closed my eyes and envisioned a different scenario. That night, after the tumor baby had been removed from my body, a masked man had snuck into the hospital, tiptoed into the operating room where it had been tossed in the garbage, and scooped it out of the bin. He had gone home, the tumor baby wrapped in a blanket and secured under his arm. The next day, he had delivered it to an orphanage for tumor babies. Several months later a couple that wanted to adopt a tumor had visited the orphanage. As soon as they had laid eyes on the tumor baby, they had known they would be taking it home. For all I knew, the tumor baby was living happily in its forever home, like the dogs I had seen on Instagram that had been rescued from animal shelters.

I rolled onto my side, straightened my arms, pressed my palms against the side of my husband. He stirred but didn't roll over. I pushed again, harder. From whatever place he went to in his dreams, he muttered a few unintelligible words. He rolled onto his side, his back to me, as I had wanted. The snoring abated.

I rolled onto my other side, my back facing his. For years I had written about sex, one purpose of which was reproduction, yet I, myself, had failed to reproduce anything but the tumor baby. In my twenties, I hadn't wanted to have kids. My mother, with her I-don't-want-to-be-a-mother-anymore mothering style, had left me with the impression that children were what prevented you from doing what you wanted to do. In my thirties, I had changed my mind: I *did* want to have kids. By then my friends had kids, and they loved their kids more than anything else, including, in some cases, their spouses. Then my husband had materialized, and it had seemed like we would adopt a kid; a boy or a girl, I didn't care, any kind of kid would do. But the tumor baby had appeared in its stead. It was hard to resent the tumor baby, though. It had been doing what babies do: growing, surviving, thriving.

Now, in the absence of a child of my own, with no kid to raise, no offspring to hug or scold or mold in one's own image, I knew that I needed to return to my writing. If I didn't do something other than cook and clean for my husband, I was afraid I would act on the self-harming impulse I had felt at the bottom of the pool.

I had told my husband about Googling the Block Project when he got home from work that evening. It had seemed to me that he had been relieved I was writing about a subject other than sex. This pattern was familiar to me. At first the guy with whom I was romantically involved would think it was *cool* that I wrote about sex. Over time, his position would shift. He got…*jealous*. There was no other word for it. It was like I was cheating on him—only I wasn't. Sex was my *beat*. But maybe if I were a husband I wouldn't want my wife, say, hanging out on a porn set talking to a male porn star with a gigantic penis. I would wish she would write about something, anything else—like gardening, or how to make an incredible lasagna in less than thirty minutes, or a personality study in which she had been a subject.

Inside the bedroom wall, a roof rat scurried up the interior. I was going to have to call the exterminator to come and block off the access point under the terra-cotta roof tile. The roof rats leaped from the palm tree onto the roof and climbed into the attic space. Once they got inside, it was hard to get rid of them.

The Block Project was as unkinky as a rest home orgy. It was *vanilla*. A human lab story, while *unusual*, could be talked about at a dinner party without offending the wives of the executives with which one's husband worked, women who didn't have careers, whose lives revolved around meeting the needs of other people, who got their nails done and chaired committees and endeavored to save the sea turtles. Ostensibly, those women *had* sex, but they didn't talk about it. More important, they didn't really like the expressions on their husbands' faces when they were informed that one of the other executives' wives wrote about sex. The roof rat scurried across the attic floor.

Perhaps I could turn over a new leaf. I could put sex writing behind me and never write another sex-related story or visit another porn set. I would no longer be a semi-serious journalist covering a salacious beat. I would be a *serious* journalist. The story about the Block Project would be my ticket to respectability. I yawned.

My husband murmured something in his sleep. It was hard to leave the past in the past, where it belonged. In the video game he played on his digital tablet, his avatar was a military tank that roared across the virtual countryside, its barrel scanning the horizon, searching for something to kill. I drifted off to sleep, forgetting everything.

On a late-summer morning, when the humidity had arrived and stepping outside felt like being swaddled in a heavy wool blanket, when all the "snowbirds"—those who spent the spring and summer up north and the fall and winter in Florida—had long since flown back home, when the streets were empty and the beachfront restaurants had closed for the season, I checked my inbox and discovered an email from the Murray Archive.

On the archive's website, I had submitted an application, requesting to see the Block Project files. I had disclosed that I was a journalist, that I was doing research, and that I had been a subject in the Blocks' study. Since then, I had worried. The archive held the data from multiple important longitudinal studies. It had rules that were designed to protect the privacy of the subjects in those studies. What if the archive's administrators thought that by looking at files that were about me, I would violate my own privacy? I wasn't sure that was possible.

I clicked on the email. It contained a password. *Yes.* I pumped my fist in the air. Finally, I was making some progress. On the Block Project page, I entered the code.

I clicked on a folder. I clicked on another folder. I clicked on another folder. Each folder contained dozens, or in some cases hundreds, of files. All told there were maybe a thousand documents, or more, I estimated. I had no idea where to begin. I clicked on a random file. I clicked on another random file. I clicked on another random file. There were scripts for interviews and instructions for tests I remembered having taken. There were acronyms I didn't understand. Charts I couldn't decipher. Mathematical calculations I failed to comprehend. Soon I was drowning in data.

In my fantasy, this scene had played out differently. I would click on a file, and my story would unfurl before me. In reality, this wasn't even a story. It was a dataset. Some of the files were in outdated formats. Others didn't open at all. I felt like an archaeologist who raises her torch to the walls of an ancient tomb and finds the impossibly coded markings of a long-dead language.

According to the archive, our dataset had been de-identified. If someone was interested in viewing the data— a researcher or a student working on a paper or a journalist—she could apply to see the files but as she went through the data she wouldn't be able to recognize its subjects. The names and other identifying information had been removed. That's how researchers protected the privacy of their subjects while sharing the hard data from their studies with others researching in the same field. But I was a subject too. On a hunch, I kept on clicking. Bit by bit, I identified a scrap of myself here, a fact from my life there. In a few hours, I had located myself in the data. But that wasn't all. At the start of the study, I had discovered, the Blocks had given each of us a three-digit number that would disguise our identity. Using the skills I had honed as a journalist, I managed to deduce my code name. I was 758.

The archive had good reason to be leery of anyone invading our privacy. Years earlier, Kaczynski had a file in the Murray Archive. Somehow his code name in Murray's study, Lawful, had been identified, and it was revealed in the press. After that, the archive had removed Kaczynski's file so no one would be able to access it. As for Kaczynski himself, he had refused to talk about his experiences as one of Murray's guinea pigs. These days, he was inmate #04475-046 at the US Penitentiary, Administrative Maximum Facility, in Fremont County, near Florence, Colorado. He occupied a cell on Bombers Row, which had housed Timothy McVeigh and Terry Nichols, the Oklahoma City bombers; Ramzi Yousef, a perpetrator of the 1993 World Trade Center bombing; and Eric Rudolph, the Olympic Park Bomber of the late 1990s.

Maybe I'll write him a letter, I pondered. *From one lab rat to another. See if I can get him to tell me about his years under Murray's microscope. Perhaps he'll write me back. We'll be pen pals. Me and the serial killer.*

I checked the time. My husband would be home from work any minute. I logged out of the archive, turned off my computer, and went to start dinner. In the kitchen, I pulled the chicken and apple sausages he liked out of the fridge. This whole time I had had another identity—another name—I hadn't known about. I was 758. Who was *she*?

I poked the sausages while they sizzled in the pan. Maybe Murray's study *had* made Kaczynski crazy. The archive sought to protect the privacy of the studies' subjects, but being in a study was all about *not* having privacy. From its first chapter, my life was an open book. My researchers had dug around inside of me, like a kid playing that game Operation, where you had to be careful while trying to remove body parts from the man's body or you would get an electric shock. It made you twitchy, to have people rutting around in your innermost places, even if their intentions were honorable. It shut you off, in a way. Maybe *I* was crazy. Maybe it was better to have some privacy. Maybe you needed a part of yourself for yourself.

As I tore lettuce into a plastic bowl for a salad, I saw my hands were shaking. I was going to have to think about something else for a while. Feelings would get in the way of my story. I had to be objective, inhabit a reporter's view from nowhere, as I had learned, even if I was the subject. In the garage, the automatic door groaned on its tracks. He was here.

"I really want to hit you, *bitch*," my husband hissed as we stood in the garage, not far from the open door. His right fist floated in the air near my head. His face was a twisted knot of rage. His eyes were black. His blue nylon athletic shirt clung to muscles that he had honed through long hours in the gym: thick trapezius, firm deltoids, bulging biceps.

If he hits me, he might kill me. Past his left shoulder I could see the driveway, the mailbox, the street. It was an ordinary August day. What would happen if one of our neighbors walked by and witnessed this tableau vivant of domestic life gone awry? We would be judged for having transgressed the first rule of suburban life: Keep your damn problems to yourself. *And they always seemed like such a nice couple*, the neighbor husband would tell the neighbor wife that evening as they ate the skirt steaks that he had cooked to perfection on their outdoor grill.

What did I do? I searched my brain for what had set him off this time. We were walking the dog, and I said something that upset him, and I couldn't recall what it was. One moment everything was fine. The next moment everything went sideways. This was the lie in our marriage I didn't want to face, ever since the time he had told me he wanted to beat the shit out of me in Illinois. Being married to him was like being trapped in a driverless car. Even when the ride was smooth you spent all your emotional energy hoping it wouldn't drive itself off a cliff.

I was dissociating, a familiar feeling. After we had moved to Florida and were still living in the apartment, he had gotten pissed off about something I had said as we had walked the dog on the side of a road. Ignoring the stream of cars, he had whirled around, raised his fist menacingly, and threatened to punch me.

"How do you like *that?*" he had asked rhetorically, gesturing like he was about to land a blow to my left temple. "Yeah, I bet you don't like *that*," he sneered.

But our marital troubles had begun long before we had relocated to the Sunshine State. Rather than addressing those problems I had ignored them, minimized them, written them off, one after the next, as if avoiding our issues would solve them, as if a new state would change his mental state, as if I could fix whatever was going on with him. But his anger hadn't eased after we moved. Under more stress at his new job, it had gotten worse.

I slipped out of my body, hovering over the scene. There was my husband, the black wedding band on his left ring finger. There was me, the diamond rings on my left ring finger. I could hear the voice of the minister who had married us in Vegas: *These rings are a symbol, a circle that binds you, a bond representing your love for one another that must never be broken.* My husband was a successful executive, a combat veteran, the one in our relationship who made all the money, something of which he regularly reminded me. *It must be my fault.*

His fist dropped. Seizing the opportunity, I turned on my heel, dashed past the DOG RULES sign (BARK SOFTLY, DO TRICKS WHEN ASKED, AND KNOW THAT I AM LOVED) that I had bought online and hung near the door, and entered the laundry room. I made a beeline through the living room and into my home office. I could hear his footsteps behind me. I sat at my desk, my hands trembling.

"Oh, no, did I upset your teacup?" he taunted from the doorway. "You're overreacting. You're so damn precious. You always make such a big deal out of everything. You know I would never hit you. You know that, right? Are you listening?"

I turned to face him.

"You scared me."

"I was *joking.*"

He disappeared. The television turned on. A man's voice delivered a play-by-play of whatever preseason football game.

I willed myself not to cry. *I can handle this*, I told myself. *I am not getting divorced and winding up like my mother*, I reminded myself. *You're overreacting*, I explained to myself.

In the bathroom, I used a wad of Kleenex to wipe away the tears. I knew the next scene. I would go in the kitchen to make dinner. He would watch the football game. At the dinner table, he would act like nothing had happened. At some point, he would make a joke. I would be relieved the storm had passed. Later, as I loaded the dishwasher, I would begin to doubt my understanding of what had happened, wondering if he had been right. *He would never hit me*, I would counsel myself. I would feel my body stiffening, turning into a woman-shaped cardboard cutout of myself. For a while, life would be normal. Then it would start again.

It was past midnight when, as my husband slept, I tiptoed out the bedroom side door that led to the pool. Being careful not to make any noise that might wake him, I opened the pool cage door and walked barefoot through the wet grass to where the backyard sloped to the fake lake. In the moonlight, I made out two otters cavorting in the lake. Their brown furry bodies glistened as they dove and resurfaced, hunting for fish, frogs, or turtles. It was in their nature to hunt. An animal couldn't help but do what it was compelled to do. I was being compelled, too.

I had to keep pursuing my story. I needed to go to California next. My mother could tell me how I had ended up in the Block Project in the first place. Piece by piece, I would put together the story of my life. Then I would know who I was meant to be.

SIX

Three weeks later, in mid-September, I was on a plane heading west. As I watched the verdant landscape slipping away far below me through the oval window, it seemed like I could see things more clearly from this bird's-eye point of view.

Bird—that's it. I was a bird in a gilded cage. I had all the trappings of the good life: a house, a partner, a BMW in a three-car garage. And once I had those things, I didn't want to lose them. For decades, I had struggled to take care of myself. It was hard to picture giving up everything. *You'll be fine,* I could hear some wiser version of me telling myself. I knew if I left my husband, I could take care of myself. But what if the breast cancer came back? *Better the devil you know than the devil you don't,* I considered. *But what if the devil kills me?* So far, my husband had only *threatened* to hit me. But what if he actually *did?* What then?

Seven hours and a flight change later, I disembarked

at Los Angeles International Airport. I rented a car and drove east on the freeway. As the overpass rose and crested above the city, I could feel my mood lifting. I *missed* LA— its surreal shininess and programmatic architecture, the promise and pathos of the sidewalk stars on Hollywood Boulevard, a place where dreams were real and anything was possible. When I got to Los Feliz, I parked across the street from the apartment complex where I had lived when I was starting out as a journalist. It seemed like a lifetime ago, another person ago. *I was so happy here*, I thought wistfully. *I wonder if I could be that happy again.*

I went north up the freeway to Burbank, where I had booked a room at a hotel. I checked in at the front desk, rode the elevator up to my room, and opened the door with the key card. I dropped my suitcase on the floor and flopped onto the bed, exhausted. I was back in the Valley. When I had lived here before, my life had been exciting. Now my life was boring. Except when my husband threatened to hit me. That was *terrifying*.

When I woke up, it was morning. I pulled on a white T-shirt and jeans. In the hotel dining room, I got in the buffet line and loaded a Styrofoam plate with dry scrambled eggs, three strips of overdone bacon, and soggy hash browns. I sat at a small table and surveyed the crowd. Three goateed guys in black T-shirts and black shorts were crewmembers on a TV show, probably. A tired-looking mom was there with her two teenage kids whom she was likely taking on the Universal Studios tour. One of the kids was a pimple-faced boy of fifteen or so who had surely seen more porn movies than I ever would and the other was a green-haired girl on her mobile phone, no doubt texting with a middle-aged pedophile she thought was a teenage boy and whom she had met in a chat room. The guy in a beige tie with a briefcase was attending a sales convention for whatever sector he was in, I theorized: aluminum siding, bouncy castles, lawn mowers.

After breakfast, I packed my black leather cross-body bag with the tools of my trade: a digital recorder, a notepad with PROFESSIONAL REPORTER'S NOTEBOOK printed on the front in case I forgot the purpose of my being there, a handful of pens. A little while later, I was barreling south on the freeway. Thankfully, the morning commuter traffic had dissipated. I pressed harder on the gas pedal.

My destination was Orange, a city a few miles southeast of Disneyland Park, in Orange County. These days, the orange groves for which the area had been named had been replaced by suburban sprawl, and it was the home of *The Real Housewives of Orange County*.

In Florida, I had tracked down George Vaillant, a renowned author, psychiatrist, and retired Harvard professor. For over thirty years, he helmed Harvard's Grant Study, which for seventy-five years followed 268 Harvard undergraduate men to find out what makes for a good life. Its cohort included President John F. Kennedy and Ben Bradlee, the *Washington Post* editor who oversaw the newspaper's investigation of the Watergate scandal. (In his memoir, *A Good Life: Newspapering and Other Adventures*, Bradlee opens with his first day in the Grant Study; "I was one of those guinea pigs," he brags.) I had sent Vaillant an email, asking if I could interview him. He had agreed.

An hour later, I was walking up a driveway to a Cape Cod–style home. After a few knocks, the front door opened. There was Vaillant: tall, sprightly, and grinning at me.

"Come in, come in!" he beckoned. His wife vanished around a corner down the hall as he escorted me through the front hallway and into an expansive and well-appointed sitting room. It smelled faintly of cat urine, I noticed as I sank into a deep cushioned cream-colored love seat. Vaillant took a seat in the bigger matching sofa across from me.

He's like Yoda, I realized. Vaillant had the I've-seen-it-all demeanor of an octogenarian. Nearby, an oversize copy of Carl Jung's *The Red Book*, in which the founder of analytical psychology chronicles his temporary descent into insanity, rested on a side table. I pressed PLAY on my recorder.

"So, what do you remember of the Blocks?" I began. I was hoping Vaillant, who had known Jack and Jeanne, could shed some light on what they had been like.

"Jack could be overbearing," Vaillant said. "Opinionated, gruff. He was combative, difficult. His father died when Jack was, before he was two, I think. Perhaps through his work he was seeking to understand how he might have been different had his father not died, how life experiences, good and bad, forge our personalities. But their study—that was, I believe, really *Jeanne's* idea. Yet when I saw them together, he seemed to *overshadow* her."

As I listened to Vaillant talk about his work in the field of longitudinal studies, I had an overwhelming urge to confess something to him that I hadn't told anyone else. Given that Vaillant was a psychiatrist, this wasn't surprising. He emitted a priestly vibe.

"I want to write this story," I told him, "but I'm not sure I'm the right person to do it. I'm a *journalist*, not a scientist. I don't have a PhD, and I'm not a psychologist. I was a *subject* in the Block Project." I paused. "I've never been the principal investigator of anything."

Vaillant dismissed my concerns with a wave.

"Susannah, none of that *matters*." He leaned forward and smiled beatifically. "You must understand one thing. Science is just stories. This is your story. You *must* tell *your* story."

You must tell your story, I thought as I drove back to the hotel. I had been here barely twenty-four hours, but already Florida and my life there seemed like a made-for-TV movie in which I had appeared but wasn't real life. As I checked the directions on my phone, I saw my husband was calling me. I put the phone in the drink holder and didn't answer it. I had to stay focused on where I was going. I turned my attention back to the road ahead of me.

———

I got up before dawn, packed my stuff, and drove to the Hollywood Burbank Airport. It was almost empty, occupied by stragglers, businesspeople, and others whose agendas I couldn't identify who were hopping on early flights to somewhere else. Less than an hour later, we landed at Oakland International Airport. I picked up a rental car and drove north. The sky was gray, oppressive. How long had it been since I had been to the Bay Area? At least a decade. A dozen years, maybe.

I got off the freeway and found my way to the Oak-land hospital where I was born. From there, I retraced the route my father would have taken from the hospital to the Child Study Center on the day of my birth. Fifteen minutes later, I was at the preschool. As I stood on the sidewalk, the sounds of children in the play yard floated over the fence. The sun broke through the clouds, illuminating the color-ful transparent trellis panels. A memory floated up from the depths of my subconscious. I was holding my mother's hand as she led me to the classroom, a rainbow at my feet.

The main door to the administrative building opened at the far end of the walkway between the buildings, snap-ping me out of my reverie. A man emerged. He was wearing glasses and a navy plaid shirt with jeans. Thirty-something. He looked like he could be a researcher studying the pre-schoolers. Midway down the walkway, he registered my presence and stiffened. He started down the ramp, ignor-ing me. When he got to the sidewalk, he gave me a wide berth, his gaze trained on the concrete. Photographers only regret the photos they didn't take. Journalists only regret the questions they didn't ask. It was now or never.

"Do you work at the preschool?" I asked as he passed me. He shook his head without looking at me and walked faster. If I didn't do something soon, he would be gone. "Are you a researcher?" I called after him.

He stopped, half turned, eyed me suspiciously.

"I went to preschool here. A long time ago," I explained and smiled.

He paused. "A lot of you come around here," he said, finally. "I have to get going." He scurried off. It was as if he was the White Rabbit from *Alice's Adventures in Wonderland* and I was Alice. *Curiouser and curiouser,* I thought, heading back to the car.

I drove along familiar streets to the hotel. There was San Francisco across the Bay, and I could see the Golden Gate in the distance. It was strange to be back in my hometown. As the plane had descended into Oakland, I had experienced a sinking feeling. This was the reason that I had stayed away for so long. Here was the place that I wanted to forget.

"I think you have a box for me."

The hotel front desk clerk went into a back room and reappeared holding the package that I had asked my husband to ship to the hotel. I wedged the box under my arm and pulled my suitcase to the elevator.

In the hotel room, I opened the bag and withdrew its contents. I sat on the bed and pulled out the tea box. I slid open the lid and lifted out the Ziploc bag. I had never been able to figure out what to do with my father's ashes. Maybe I could now. I put the bag back in the tea box and the tea box on the table next to the coffeemaker.

Daddy issues. Apparently, I had them. But what did that even *mean?* It was a term for a woman who had unresolved issues stemming from her relationship with her father when she was a little girl. My father was there. Then he was not. He had left my mother, but he had also left me—*with her.* She had been unhappy, and when he wasn't around, I had felt like it had been my job to make her happy. But that hadn't been my job. I had been a *child.*

Years later, when I had set foot in that first strip club,

and I had shown up on that first porn movie set, I had wanted to be like the women at the center of the action. In my eyes, they were powerful, beautiful, liberated. In other words, those women were everything my mother wasn't. Over the years, a more nuanced picture had emerged. Those women *looked* empowered, but the men ran the show, from the strip club owners to the porn directors to the CEOs of the tube sites that had gobbled up the porn companies that produced most of the content.

In 2009, when I was living in Virginia, I had traveled to LA and spent a week reporting a 10,000-word story about the Great Recession's impact on the adult movie business. (The previous year's economic crisis had catastrophically hobbled the porn industry, already weakened by the spread of its own pirated content online and a string of federal obscenity indictments.) I knew I was on the right track when I pulled into the parking lot of the Hollywood Roosevelt Hotel and espied Ron "The Hedgehog" Jeremy waiting for the valet to retrieve his car. I ended up in a Woodland Hills mansion that had been rented for the day for the sole purpose of shooting a porn movie. In the living room, I watched a girl hanging from a swing suspended from the ceiling copulate with a dildo attached to a metal prong connected to a motor that thrust the dildo back and forth. The pretty, tan, brunette, twenty-something star resembled a young Sandra Bullock. When I asked her why she got into porn, she shrugged and replied: "For money."

It had been nearly a dozen years since the orgy on the fire truck. In that mansion, I knew what I had to do to get the story I wanted—which is to say the *real* story. On the sofa, I sat with my legs apart, manspreading. The PA made a dirty joke; I laughed. Near the end, it was time for the girl to switch from vaginal to anal, and she choked, teary-eyed, "I think I'm gonna cry." I said, did nothing, resisting any impulse I might have had to ally myself with her. I didn't want to be one of the girls. I wanted to be *one of the guys*. That's where the power was.

On the morning of my second day, I crossed Sproul Plaza. My father's cremains were in my bag. At Wheeler, where my father had an office when he was an English professor, I walked around the building. I debated sprinkling his ashes in the shrubs. Someone might call the campus police to report a possible terrorist act in progress, so I decided against it. I went in the building through a north-side door and trotted up the stairs to the top floor. I wandered in a circle until I found his old office. A woman's name was posted next to the door. I cupped my hands around my eyes and peered through the smoked glass. All I could see were shadowy outlines, indistinct forms.

I headed for the stairs. A student with a neon-pink ponytail went ahead of me. SO IT GOES, a cursive tattoo at the nape of her neck read. It was a line from Kurt Vonnegut's *Slaughterhouse-Five, or, The Children's Crusade: A Duty-Dance with Death*. In the 1969 semi-autobiographical novel, Billy Pilgrim, a soldier who was a prisoner of war in Dresden when it was bombed during World War II and who has "become unstuck in time," meets aliens from a planet called Tralfamadore. These beings, he learns, experience the past, present, and future simultaneously. Tralfamadorians don't believe in death. To them, a person is always alive and dead at the same time. The line "so it goes" is repeated throughout the book in a nod to the inevitability, even banality of death.

So it goes, I thought.

When I got back to my rental car, I put my father's cremains back in the tea box and the tea box on the back seat. Next I was going to Santa Cruz, where I had arranged to meet with Per Gjerde, a retired University of California, Santa Cruz, psychology professor, who had joined the Block Project in 1978. After Jeanne died, Gjerde had become Jack's right-hand man. When I had reached him by phone, the first thing I had asked was if he remembered me.

"I remember your *name!*" he had replied in a thick Norwegian accent.

An hour-and-a-half drive later, I was sitting at Gjerde's dining room table. He was tall, oval-faced, in his early seventies. He seemed faintly familiar.

"Children *like* to be under study," he was enthusing. "It make them feel *special.*" I nodded appreciatively. Gjerde understood what it had been like for us kids in the cohort. He *got* it. Together, he and Jack had harvested our data. Over the years, the men coauthored several scientific papers about us, some of which I found online and had read.

I recounted what had happened with the M&M's: how I had wanted the candy but declined it, how the examiner had left the room, how I had gobbled them up.

"Yes!" He gestured in agreement. "We did that on *purpose*. It *was* a test of your ability to delay gratification. This was our version of Mischel's marshmallow test."

Presumably, I had failed. My ability-to-delay-gratification score: 0.

"I've read a lot of the published papers about our study, Per," I said. "But I wanted to ask you: *Did* you—the *study*, that is—predict who I—that is, *we* would grow up to be?"

"Well, this research was very forward-looking for its time." He hesitated, thinking. "It is a complicated question. In many ways, the answer was, yes, yes, we could. When you were teenagers, the ones of you who got depressed, or you were experimenting with the drugs, we had seen indicators these things would happen from when you were young: three, four years of age. Your personalities were like a road map, we could say. This study was impressive in that regard. You did something *important*. You proved it is possible to see who we will be."

As my rental car climbed up the Santa Cruz Mountains, I thought about what Gjerde had told me. In a small way, I had played a role in enlightening humanity. But I hadn't been special, as I had wanted to believe as a kid. That had been the wish of a lonely girl, for whom attention had felt like love. As my mother had told me: Wishes aren't reality. In truth, I had been little more than a data point among other data points on someone else's spreadsheet.

So it goes, I thought, the hills rising above me.

———

"You look exactly the same!" my mother declared. I had called her after I arrived in the Bay Area. Now I was on her porch. She looked the same, too, for the most part. Her hair was grayer, and she had shrunk an inch or so. From behind her glasses, she appraised me with her usual cool, analytical squint. She gave me a brief hug. I followed her inside.

"Are you hungry? I made a cheese plate. And salad. I put together some sandwiches. Sliced turkey. With Asiago. And tomato. On a Semifreddi's seeded baguette. You have this one. I'll have this one. Do you want juice?"

We settled down for lunch at her dining room table. Through the French doors, I could see the hot tub over which there were hanging flower baskets she had planted with pansies and lobelias and begonias. Around the corner, past the deck, there was a small studio for writing, although I didn't know how much writing she was doing nowadays. At one point, she had had a book deal with the University of California Press to write a biography of the objectivist poet Lorine Niedecker, but she had never written it. *I'm like a hummingbird, flitting from flower to flower!* she had explained, although I wasn't sure what that meant. I suspected she had gotten bored with it. Or maybe it had been too hard.

"Tell me about your life."

"I'm married, and—"

"What does he do?"

"He does strategy, mergers and acquisitions, and—"

"I don't even know what that means!" Likely she did know. This was a swipe at my husband. In her world, non-academics were less than academics. It didn't matter who you were or what you did, if you weren't an intellectual, you weren't worthy. *Maybe that's why I ended up writing about porn*, I considered. *It's not exactly academic.* In Porn Valley, I didn't have to spout Lacanian theory or debate semiotics or parse Molly Bloom's soliloquy at the end of James Joyce's *Ulysses* in order to be deemed worthy. (Not that there was anything wrong with *Ulysses*, but I would rather enjoy it than analyze it, especially its incandescent, onanistic climax: "yes I said yes I will Yes.") I made a mental note to not confess the troubles in my marriage. That would only give her the satisfaction that I had proved her right: *Never get married!*

"He does business deals. We got married in—"

"Would you say he is...self-aware?"

"Um, I, well—"

"He doesn't *sound* very self-aware."

I wasn't sure what to do with this comment.

"We bought a house. In Florida. It's very nice. We have a pool."

She pursed her lips and said nothing. I gathered she had an impression of what houses in Florida looked like, and it was not positive. If my life was a test, it seemed, I had failed to meet her expectations of me. In her mind, I was supposed to be reading books or writing books or teaching at an academic institution or being an intellectual with other intellectual folks. But that's not what *I* had wanted. *I* had wanted to be where the action was.

My mother said, "I don't understand why we don't talk."

I opened my mouth and closed it.

Where to begin? The hurricane—that would do it. But I didn't want to go there, to have to hear her reasoning as to why she hadn't called me to find out if I had survived it. First, she would deny that version of events. Then she would obfuscate her role in the narrative. She would toss in a pinch of misdirection or a soupçon of disinformation. For her penultimate move, I would be made to blame. And then for the big finale she would stop talking again, meaning: The case was closed.

"I feel so bad about you having breast cancer." She had read what I wrote online about my diagnosis. "I wish I had been there for you. I feel very badly." Her eyes watered.

When I was living in New Orleans, I had gone to see her and my grandmother and my sister in Pennsylvania for Christmas. My grandfather had died a year or so earlier, and my grandmother was in the assisted living residence to which they had moved as they had gotten older. We had layered on coats and hats and scarves to go to the mall or antiques shopping or get donuts, and I had made a comment that annoyed my mother. I was being impatient, or sarcastic, or pseudo-witty. Around this time, my mother had decided to stop taking Prozac, for some reason or other, she hadn't really explained, and instead of doing so under a doctor's supervision, as I thought you were supposed to do, she had done it on her own, and cold turkey.

Infuriated by whatever I had said, she had grabbed the ends of the scarf around my neck and pulled them in opposite directions, as if choking me. It wasn't that she had pantomimed strangling me that was disturbing; it was her expression as she had done it. In her physical proximity to her mother who had done unkind things to her, or because of Prozac withdrawal, or due to something about me—my father's genes?—she didn't like, she had let her mask slip. A wave of feeling had washed across her typically stony face: a seething resentment, an unbridled bitterness, a primal rage.

"I'm all better now," I said, to make her feel better. I didn't want a repeat of what had happened in Pennsylvania. It was best to keep a detached distance from my mother, I had learned, as if, say, one were to wake up one morning to discover a wolf had moved into one's kitchen. I placed my recorder on the table between us and guided her to the subject of the Block Project, shifting my mindset into a more clinical I'm-a-reporter mode.

"Whose idea was it to put me in the preschool and the study?"

"It was *mine.*" She folded her arms protectively across her body. I had thought it was my father's idea; in my mind, that had meant he thought I was special. Seemingly, I had been wrong. Cocking her head, she gazed out the window. A smirk danced across her lips. "I wanted more time for *myself!* I was working. I had things to do. You girls were *a lot.* I needed time to breathe. It was *really* hard. Your father was *always* writing. I wanted my own life. Is that *wrong?*"

As my mother continued to talk about how hard being a mother was, my thoughts drifted to the tumor baby. It would be three and a half now. Probably preparing to start preschool, one in which it wouldn't be enrolled in a psychological experiment. I wondered if it ever missed me, woke up in the middle of the night crying for me, longed for the thick, sinewy, damp confines of my breast tissue. Considering my mother's relationship to mothering me, perhaps it was for the best I had never had kids. I might have resented them as much as she did me for their imposition. As she droned on, it occurred to me that I had gotten everything I was going to get.

"I have some of Dad's ashes. I don't know what to do with them," I told her before I left. Maybe she could do this one thing for me. "I thought maybe you would." I produced the box from my bag and handed it to her. She opened the box and held up the bag, inspecting it, smiling. There was triumph in that smile. *I'm still winning, you bastard!* she was thinking.

In a few weeks' time, I would get an email from my mother. She had driven to a beach north of the Bay Area, she wrote, and tossed my father's ashes into the churning waves. Finally, she had disposed of the last remaining bit of him. Afterward, she added, she felt better.

———

I flew back to Florida. My trip to the Bay Area left me depressed. I thought my life had been one way; in fact, it had been another. I wished I had never begun digging around in my past; that I had let the proverbial sleeping dogs lie. I put my brain on autopilot, tried not to think about much of anything, and stayed married. In this manner, a year and a half passed.

Then, on a spring afternoon in 2017, I drove up Highway 41, heading north for a doctor's office where I had an appointment for my annual mammogram. Five years had gone by since I had been diagnosed with breast cancer. This was, my oncologist had said, the amount of time after which it was unlikely that my breast cancer would return.

In the changing room, I put on a long pink smock. Before I left, I snapped a selfie in the mirror to mark this momentous occasion. Because of my breast cancer history, I was scheduled for a mammogram and a breast ultrasound; my radiologist would have a thorough view of my breast tissue.

The mammogram went smoothly. For the breast ultrasound, I lay on the examining room table with my right arm tucked behind my head. The technician smeared cold lube across my right breast and commenced pushing the ultrasound machine's transducer back and forth across my skin. Over and over, she returned to the area of my right breast where the tumor had been. My palms started to sweat. My throat began to constrict. My chest grew tighter.

"I'm going to share your results with the doctor."

The last image remained on the monitor. I couldn't miss the nickel-size black spot amid the cobweb of white tissue. I felt like I was going to pass out. *If it comes back,* my oncologist had told me, *we can treat you, but there may be nothing more we can do for you.*

My thoughts raced toward what would come next. There would be more operations, more rounds of chemo, more rads. All my hair would fall out again, and my brain would turn to mush once more, and the husband I was so desperately trying to hang on to would recoil at the sight of me, because who wanted to be married to a malignancy? No one.

The technician appeared at the exam room door. I followed her down the hallway to the radiologist's office at the other end. She knocked on the door.

"Come in."

The radiologist was studying my scans at a long desk in her dimly lit office. She motioned for me to take a seat beside her. I sat there quietly as she muttered to herself. Her brow was furrowed. *That is cancer,* she was going to say.

"It's a cyst," she announced. "It's benign."

"So, I'm...totally fine?"

"Yup."

As I drove past the country clubs, pickleball courts, and shrimp shacks, I wondered how many second chances I was going to be afforded before I ran out of chances, how many days I was going to spend being unhappy before I ran out of days, how much more time I was going to waste before my time ran out.

I parked in our garage and went inside. I chucked my bag on the kitchen counter and went to the sliding glass doors. Past the pool cage, an arc of water ejaculated out of the fake lake. I wanted more than a house made of cinder blocks, a view of a lake that wasn't real, and a husband who threatened to hit me. The moment had come. If I wanted my life to be different than it was, I was going to have to stop running from the truth and start facing it.

When my husband got home from work, I was waiting for him.

"Things have to change," I told him.

"I want a divorce," he declared.

In his eyes, I could see tiny versions of myself reflected back at me. To make this man love me, I had made myself smaller and smaller. One day, I would disappear altogether.

"Okay," I said, knowing it was over.

SEVEN

T hat night, I slept in the primary bedroom and he slept in the guest bedroom on the other side of the house. The next morning, I waited until I heard the garage door close after he had driven off for work. Once I had made sure he was gone, I started a pot of coffee and got down to work in my home office. I had to find a divorce attorney, but that would have to wait.

A few days before, I had received an email that included a link to a 1980 episode of the long-running science documentary series *Nova*, titled "The Pinks and the Blues," about how gender roles are formed. I clicked the link to the episode. The video started. Twenty minutes later, Jack and Jeanne appeared on my computer screen, sitting side by side as they watched a video on a monitor of two boys playing at the Child Study Center. They laughed at something on the monitor. She smiled, looked at him. He grinned, his eyes on the monitor. My principal investigators had been resurrected. Florida faded into the background.

According to the Blocks' two-factor theory of personality, ego-control and ego-resiliency are personality characteristics that shape our emotions, motivations, and behaviors. Ego-control is the degree to which we express or inhibit our impulses; ego-resiliency is the degree to which we express or inhibit our impulses based on social demands. Starting in preschool, our ego-control had been measured on a spectrum ranging from "undercontrolled" to "overcontrolled." If we were spontaneous, comfortable with ambiguity, and emotionally expressive, we were *undercontrolled*; if we were disciplined, uncomfortable with uncertainty, and emotionally unexpressive, we were *overcontrolled*. Our ego-resiliency had been measured on a spectrum, as well. If we adapted easily to change, engaged or relaxed depending on the situation, and accommodated and assimilated others, we scored high in resiliency. If we were inflexible, disturbed by change, and slow to recover from traumatic events, we scored low in resiliency. (In all likelihood, I mused, I was an undercontroller and my husband was an overcontroller; or, put another way, we were doomed.) Over the years, those of us who were undercontrolled remained undercontrolled, and those of us who were overcontrolled remained overcontrolled. In other words, you could predict, to some degree, what kind of person a child would grow up to be.

But our personalities weren't fixed, they had discovered. Our parents and other life factors played a role in shaping us. One of those life factors was gender. The Blocks hadn't set out to study sex role differences, but early on Jeanne had observed that the boys and girls in our cohort behaved differently. Was it nature? Was it nurture? Was it both?

Our parents, despite their best intentions, treated us differently, depending on our gender, Jeanne had learned. While the boys were encouraged to be independent, the girls were encouraged to be compliant. While the boys were encouraged to roam, the girls were encouraged to stay close. While the boys were encouraged to experiment, the girls weren't. While the boys were taught to compete, the girls were taught to collaborate. In school, our teachers reinforced the message. In the classroom, the boys' successes were more likely to be attributed to ability while the girls' successes were more likely to be attributed to luck. While the boys were taught to believe in themselves, the girls were taught to doubt themselves. While the boys learned to blame their failures on external circumstances, the girls learned to blame their failures on themselves. *Touché*, I thought.

I had come of age in (arguably) the most liberal city in America. My mother claimed to have read Betty Friedan's *The Feminine Mystique* while pushing a vacuum cleaner. My father had led me to believe I could do anything as well as a boy could do if not better. Yet somewhere along the way, I had learned to doubt myself, second-guess myself, undervalue myself. I could blame the patriarchy or misogyny, my parents or my teachers, *Cinderella* or Barbie, but in the end I had made every single choice that had brought me to this place. *If the world can change who I am, can I change myself into the person I want to be, who doesn't doubt herself, who values herself, who's happy and fulfilled and feels worthy?* I wondered.

Coco barked, demanding a walk. In the garage, I put on her leash. As she dragged me down the sidewalk the sun seemed brighter, the sky bluer, the grass greener. My marriage had shit the bed, but my story was cohering. I wasn't a failure, a fuckup, a bad wife. I was the result of signals and messages, covert and overt, that had reshaped who I was into someone I did not want to be. Bending over so far backward to please a man that I had thought my spine would crack, expecting less for myself, discerning my needs were less important than someone else's.

The dog squatted over the grass, excreting a turd, panting with the effort of elimination. This was more than a personal story. It was a psychological experiment of my own, one in which I was my own research subject. I pulled a plastic bag over my hand, snagged the warm dog poop, and tied the bag's top into a knot. I scampered back to the house.

On my computer, I Googled: *What are the steps of an experiment?*

1. **Make an observation.** In my notebook, I wrote: *I'm not who I want to be.*
2. **Ask a question.** I jotted down: *How did I become who I am?*
3. **Form a hypothesis.** I chewed my nail. This one was important: *If I can figure out how I became who I am, I can become who I want to be.*
4. **Make a prediction based on the hypothesis.** I scratched my head. *If I can figure out how I became who I am, I can become who I want to be, and I will be the real me.*

5. **Test the prediction.** I frowned. I had to get out of here to do that.

Jeanne had seen what was going to happen to us girls before anyone else had. I wouldn't let her hard work go to waste. If she was right, I could use it to change my life.

———————

A few weeks later, I had an appointment with a divorce attorney. In the garage, I cut open the top of an old cardboard box of my saved stuff with a pair of scissors, trying not to think about the retainer I'd paid her. The box was filled with random ephemera: a 1970s-era Super 8 film camera that my sister and I had used to make home movies; a flattened pale-blue teddy bear with a rose behind its ear that had been mine when I was a baby; essays and short stories I had written in college. From the detritus, I plucked an unmarked large white envelope.

Inside, there was a letter from Jack to me, dated June 23, 1989. With it, there were: an article about the Block Project; scientific papers based on the study (among them: "Parental Agreement-Disagreement on Child-Rearing Orientations and Gender-Related Personality Correlates in Children," "Longitudinally Foretelling Drug Usage in Adolescence: Early Childhood Personality and Environmental Precursors," and "Testing Aspects of Carl Rogers's Theory of Creative Environments: Child-Rearing Antecedents of Creative Potential in Young Adolescents"); an eight-page, double-sided list of articles, papers, and graduate and doctoral student theses about us, including "The Eysencks and Psychoticism," from the *Journal of Abnormal Psychology*; "Fire and Young Children: A Study of Attitudes, Behaviors, and Maternal Teaching Strategies," a report for the Pacific Southwest Forest and Range Experiment Station; and "Growing Up in a Scary World," a 16-millimeter film that had been produced for UC Berkeley. *Scary world, indeed.*

I recognized the University of California letterhead on Jack's letter. My father had used the same letterhead. The university's official seal, which was designed by Tiffany & Co. at the turn of the twentieth century, featured an open book signifying knowledge. Under that, a curling banner read: LET THERE BE LIGHT.

"Dear Susannah," the letter began. It was a form letter; the others had gotten one too. He had wanted to know if I would be willing to participate in their next assessment. This was no small request. The assessments were long, probing, intimate. Their subject matter was deeply personal, a thorough inventorying of our private lives and psyches. No subject was off-limits: drug abuse and depression, sex and suicide, divorce and death. Jack seemed to understand the impact, noting that while a great deal had been asked of us in the previous assessments, our sacrifice was worth it. "I believe you will find it personally helpful to participate in the forthcoming assessment, now in its final planning stages," he wrote. "I am certain your participation will improve the scientific understanding of why people turn out as they do."

As I read the last sentence, I was reminded of how I had felt when I was in the study: like I was special, like my life had a greater meaning, like I had a *higher purpose*. But maybe the study hadn't been my higher purpose. Maybe the story I was working on now—my story—was.

Back at my computer a few hours later, I read about the time the Block Project made headlines in 2006. The previous year, Jack published a scientific paper (posthumously co-credited to Jeanne) in the *Journal of Research in Personality* titled "Nursery School Personality and Political Orientation Two Decades Later." In the paper, Jack claimed those of us who were "self-reliant, energetic, somewhat dominating, relatively under-controlled, and resilient" as preschoolers grew up to be politically liberal as adults, and those of us who were "indecisive, fearful, rigid, inhibited, and relatively over-controlled and vulnerable" as preschoolers grew up to be politically conservative as adults.

Outraged conservatives had dismissed the findings as liberal propaganda and Jack as a quack. "I really shouldn't be happy—because I'm a Republican," conservative commentator Glenn Beck had mockingly told his millions of viewers on the premiere of his eponymous CNN show. WERE CONSERVATIVES WHINY CHILDREN? a headline had queried. GUESS WHAT CONSERVATIVES ARE WHINY BRATS, a message board thread had shouted. "I found it to be biased, shoddy work, poor science at best," University of Arizona social psychology professor Jeff Greenberg had sniffed to the *Toronto Star*.

On the internet, I tracked down a PDF of the paper that had caused the uproar. In a footnote, I noticed, Jack had thanked a Peter Feld "for help in computer analyses." Curious, I found Feld's email address and sent him a note, asking him if he would speak to me. He responded, saying he would be happy to talk. When I reached him by phone, he related that he had worked on the Block Project at UC Berkeley. Peter had been the one who had analyzed our data to find out if there was a relationship between our preschool personality traits and our adult political orientation. He had written up his findings as his dissertation, but he had never published his work. There was a "deep flaw in the data," he explained. "There were a lot of things where it didn't matter that you guys were in Berkeley, but for political attitudes, it did matter." Many of our parents had leaned left. To draw any broader conclusions, more research would have needed to be done with a cohort that had more politically diverse backgrounds.

After Jack had died, Peter had heard from his cousin, who had read Jack's *New York Times* obituary, which had cited the political orientation findings paper. It seemed as if Jack had taken Peter's analyses and conclusions, published Peter's work as if it had been his own, and failed to address the problematic aspect of our liberal-leaning upbringings.

I thanked Peter and hung up. Had Jack ripped off his protégé's hard work? Had he ignored the complexity behind the science to make a newsworthy splash? By then, Jack had been in his eighties and had retired. Maybe he had worried that if he didn't publish *something*, his life's work would have ended up relegated to the ash heap of history.

I had thought I had been part of an important study of personality. Heck, I had willingly sacrificed my privacy at the altar of their scientific inquiry. But this plot twist wasn't one I had expected. Was this how science worked…or was this smoke and mirrors?

Every weekday after my ex-husband-to-be left for work, I kept throwing myself into my research. (On weekends, I stayed out of the house as much as I could, going to a local movie theater, where I bought tickets to whatever matinee featured a powerful female main character, like *Wonder Woman* or *Atomic Blonde*, in which an ice-blond, reed-thin Charlize Theron plays an undercover MI6 agent who beats the crap out of every man who tries to stop her from completing her mission.) It was as if I had entered into a sort of cosmic loop. By traveling back into my past, I was beginning to understand my present.

Gjerde, whom I had talked to in Santa Cruz, had been interested in the roots of depression. As he had told me, they had been able to see signs in early childhood of which of us would spiral into depression when we reached adolescence. The boys most at risk for later depression had been marked by aggression. The girls most at risk for later depression had sounded a lot like a young me: smart, kind (well, mostly), and shy.

Online, I download the 1995 paper Gjerde had written about us that had focused on girls and depression and been published in the scientific journal *Child Development*. In "Alternative Pathways to Chronic Depressive Symptoms in Young Adults: Gender Differences in Developmental

Trajectories," I read how the girls in our cohort who were smart and confident (even if also shy), of which I had been one, became sad young women. When we reached puberty we realized we were a deviation from the norm. Society had defined what a girl could be—and smart and confident wasn't on the list. To fit in, we concealed our intelligence and competed less; I did this in grade school. Hiding our true identities, we turned melancholic; this happened to me, too. To us, the broader social construct of what a girl "should" be was overwhelming. The same wasn't true for boys. The boys were allowed to be smart and ambitious at any age. But for girls like me, being smart and confident wasn't an asset. It was a *problem.*

In our teens, girls who were strong-willed, who weren't eager to please, who were brainy and bold, spiraled into depression. Girls like me were deviants, freaks, weirdos.

In fact, I had learned, a dirty little secret of human subject research was that its subjects didn't represent most people. Overwhelmingly, we were from Western, Educated, Industrialized, Rich, and Democratic societies— or WEIRD. According to an article I read, "The Weirdest People in the World?," which appeared in *Behavioral and Brain Sciences*, a peer-reviewed journal published by Cambridge University Press, in 2010, and was coauthored by Joseph Henrich, Steven J. Heine, and Ara Norenzayan of the University of British Columbia, an analysis of the top psychology journals published between 2003 and 2007 revealed that 68 percent of the research subjects were from the United States, and 96 percent were from Western industrialized nations. Of the US subjects, 67 percent were undergraduate students enrolled in psychology courses. Furthermore, research subjects from those Western industrialized nations, which represented only 12 percent of the world's population, were uniquely *un*representative of people in general, differing from the global population across a wide range of factors, including moral reasoning, visual perception, and cooperation. And it wasn't just the adults. The children who were research subjects in studies were no more representative of most children than the adults who were research subjects in studies were representative of most adults.

"The findings suggest that members of WEIRD societies, including young children," the authors had concluded, "are among the least representative populations one could find for generalizing about humans."

When I was in Berkeley, I had toured the Child Study Center. In the classroom, which I was permitted to enter when the children were outside, I remembered what it was like to be there as a preschooler. To four-year-old me, it was a magical place. In his design, Esherick had privileged the needs of the children over the needs of the adults. The three-foot-tall cubby area where we stored our belongings was situated at our eye level. The soaring ceilings diminished the height difference between the adults and us, making us feel less small, more equal. The two-story playhouse's low ceiling prevented adults from entering our kids-only space. On the south side of the classroom, the tall windows filled the room with sunlight, and the orange window frames dissolved the barrier between indoors and outdoors, promoting our self-directed play and our independent exploration of the environment.

But I had thought of a paper I had read, "The Panopticon of Childhood," which was published in *Paedagogica Historica* in 2005 and written by Ning de Coninck-Smith, a professor at the Danish School of Education at Aarhus University in Aarhus, Demark. It had offered up a darker take. To de Coninck-Smith's eye, the Child Study Center was a panopticon, a type of industrial building conceived by the English social theorist Jeremy Bentham in the late eighteenth century. In the panopticon-as-prison, a guard occupies a central tower from which he can see into all the prison cells and into which no prisoner can see. As a result, the prisoner internalizes his or her own surveillance. As a consequence, the guard's control is total. "Is our research into children for their sake or for the sake of the adults?" she asked. "And is it possible to combine consideration for research with respect for the individual—even when that individual is a child?" At the preschool, she asserted, privacy "was an illusion—at least, if you were a child."

In an interview with Esherick I had retrieved from an online archive, he recalled visiting the preschool at its first location on campus while working on the designs for its new home. There, the teachers assured him the children had *no idea* they were being studied. Ensconced in the pavilion that overlooked the yard, he peered through the screen. It was a window into the secret lives of children. As he looked on, one child pinched another child until the child cried, but when the teacher appeared, the pincher feigned innocence, and the teacher was none the wiser.

On another visit, however, he noticed a little girl linger-ing near the pavilion. As the other children filed inside, she began to pound the side of the pavilion in which he was hiding with her tiny fists. "I know you're in there!" she hollered. So perhaps the children weren't so unaware after all. Years later, Esherick confessed, he remained conflicted about the Child Study Center. "I never liked all this hidden stuff," he confided to the interviewer. "It seemed too Big Brother–ish to me."

The more I read, the more questions I had. It seemed like there was good research and bad research, representa-tive subjects and unrepresentative subjects, claims of objec-tivity and the observer effect at work. I hadn't known I was being spied on the preschool—or had I? Science was sup-posed to be the absolute truth. In fact, it seemed like the truth was a mystery.

———————

On the TV in the living room, Hurricane Irma, a Category 5 case of déjà vu, swirled toward Southwest Florida, where a hurricane of that size hadn't made landfall in over a decade. Since we had agreed to divorce six months earlier, I had stayed in the house as our attorneys had negotiated the terms of our marital settlement agreement. My ex-to-be wanted me out, but I knew I was in a better position to negotiate if I didn't leave. He was enraged I wasn't doing what I had done before: give up, give in, give him what-ever he wanted. For the first time, I had dug in my heels and stood my ground. I locked the bedroom door at night, came out after he went to work, and kept a knife in the top drawer of the nightstand in case the situation escalated. Sure, it was stupid, reckless, dangerous. I was playing with fire, almost daring him to do something, but I was tired of him pushing me around. My position on the matter: *Fuck him.* As the Mexican revolutionary Emiliano Zapata said, "It is better to die on your feet than to live on your knees." I had joked to a girlfriend: "The only thing that'll push me out of this house is a Category 5 hurricane." Mother Nature had accepted my challenge.

Given the devastation Hurricane Katrina had wrought in New Orleans, I wasn't about to hang around and find out if the storm would make a direct hit. I decided to go to Memphis; I had never been to Tennessee. I hopped on a plane packed with folks fleeing the hurricane, and after deplaning at the Memphis International Airport, I rented a car and drove to a downtown hotel. I left my bags in the room and walked toward the Mississippi River. Away from the war zone of our house, I felt myself decompressing from the stress as I walked along the riverbank. One day, I reminded myself, the marital settlement agreement would be signed, the divorce would be finalized, and Florida would be rapidly diminishing in the rear-view mirror.

That week I went to Gus's World Famous Fried Chicken, where I ate the best fried chicken I had ever eaten, baked beans, and coleslaw. I went to Graceland, where I toured Elvis's mansion, admired his bejeweled costumes and private jets, and ate his favorite sandwich (peanut butter, banana, and bacon) at the diner. I followed Interstate 55 south and then US Route 278 to Oxford, Mississippi, where I visited Rowan Oak, the estate of my favorite writer, William Faulkner. In a back room in the main house I admired how upon the walls he had scrawled the outline of his 1954 novel *A Fable*, for which he would win the Pulitzer Prize and the National Book Award. As I stared at his handwritten words, I thought my heart might burst at the beauty of it all, how you could have a story in your head and write it into the world so everyone else could bear witness to it too.

September was almost over when I signed the settlement agreement at the end of an eleven-and-a-half-hour formal mediation. My ex-to-be and I sat in two separate meeting rooms at my divorce attorney's office while the mediator shuttled back and forth between the two. Afterward, as I waited for him to leave, I could hear my ex-to-be joking around with my attorney in the hall. He wanted everyone to think he had come out on top. But I no longer had to care what he wanted. I had lost my marriage and won my freedom.

That night I took the boxes of my belongings to the house of a friend who was going to ship them to me once I had found a place to live in LA. When I returned to the house, I noticed my ex had moved his things out of his home office and into mine. I hadn't left yet, and already it was as if I had never even existed.

I went in the primary bedroom to get the rest of my stuff and locked the door. In an abusive relationship, I knew, the victim is most in danger when she's leaving. I could tell he had been in the room—he had moved around my things. I opened the nightstand drawer. The knife I had placed there to protect myself was gone. My heart pounded in my chest.

I grabbed my bags and slipped out the side door. In the driveway, I tossed my suitcases into the back seat of my car. Then I sped off into the darkness, to start over, to test my hypothesis, to become whoever I was meant to be.

————————

As the plane sailed west, I closed my eyes. I wondered what ~~my husband~~—my *ex*-husband was doing. Enjoying his breakfast in ~~our~~—*his* kitchen nook. Paddling around in ~~our~~—*his* backyard pool. Working at ~~my~~—*his* desk in ~~my~~—*his* home office. But I no longer had to give a shit about him, what he was doing, what he was thinking. No more being married to him, no more guessing what might set him off next, no more wondering when he would raise his fist as if about to punch me in the head again. Those days were over, behind me, gone and done. I was a free woman, our divorce finalized, courtesy of a family court judge I had never met in a state I had put behind me.

When I opened my eyes, the plane's strong humming had quieted to a dull vibration, and the view through the window had bifurcated: the blue sky above, the white cloud layer below. The Gulf of Mexico was down there somewhere, serene and still. Throughout the grueling process of the divorce, I had envisioned this moment, trying to imagine how I would feel, once I was free of him: thrilled, excited, emancipated. But I didn't feel any of those things. Instead, I felt empty. I wondered if there was something wrong with me, and if so what that something was, and if the something that was wrong with me was curable or fatal.

I have post-traumatic marriage disorder, I determined. If a soldier could get post-traumatic stress disorder from being in a war, couldn't a woman get post-traumatic marriage disorder from being married to an asshole? Our marriage had been the battleground. I had felt my ex was the unpredictable danger. His toxic behavior had been the cause of my trauma. My self-diagnosed condition couldn't be found in the *Diagnostic and Statistical Manual of Mental Disorders,* but that didn't make it any less real, not to me, the one who had it.

I had a textbook case of depersonalization or derealization, but those polysyllabic words weren't going to fix me. I took another sip of the orange juice I had spiked with the miniature bottle of vodka I had bought from the flight attendant for seven bucks. Maybe what I really needed was a lobotomy, for someone to drill a hole in my skull to release the bad memories. Or maybe a drive-thru round of electroshock therapy.

At some point I would have to call my mother and tell her that my marriage had ended. How many times had she told me never to marry? Too many times to count. Yet I had ignored her instructions and done it anyway. *I told you so!* she would think but not say. I made a mental note to put that conversation off as long as I could.

From my bag, I pulled out the latest issue of *Vogue,* which I had bought at the airport. On the cover, a famous actress was wearing a rose-and-black Victorian gown with a high collar and looking pensive while standing in a rowboat. *Not very relatable, unless, of course, you hang around in fancy dresses in paddleboats.* On the glossy pages, there were Photoshopped faces, digitally lengthened legs, impossibly pert derrieres. If this was what a woman was supposed to look like, I was coming up short. I had one so-so, uncut breast, and one boob that was smaller than the other that I had named my zombie boob. In addition to the chunk that had been taken out of my right breast, there was a scar where the port-a-cath had been on the left side of my chest and a scar in my right armpit from where a couple of lymph nodes had been removed for dissection to identify if they were cancerous (they weren't). The rest of me was different, too. I had a boyishly short haircut to conceal that after chemo my hair had grown back thinner. Combined with my height, it caused me to be mistaken for a man at least once a week. I closed the magazine and stuffed it in the pocket on the back of the seat in front of me, sandwiching it between a *Hemispheres Magazine* and a barf bag.

The booze and the low whoosh of the airplane lulled me into a fitful sleep, and I dreamed I was in the bathroom of the Vegas chapel in which we had gotten married. I was wearing my wedding gown. I was holding the bouquet of roses. *Are you coming?* my husband asked from the other side of the bathroom door. *Are you coming?* he asked again, louder. I stepped backward. At the other end of the bathroom, there was a small window. I could fit my body through the opening and escape. *Are you coming?* my husband shouted, banging his fists against the door. At the window, I got up onto my tiptoes. Outside, there was a field that I could run through on my way to someplace else. *Are you coming?* my husband screamed, the door hinges rattling. *If I don't leave now, he will swallow me whole,* I realized as the bathroom door crashed open.

In the plane's bathroom, I splashed cold water on my face. *You've got to keep it together.* There was no Prince Charming 2.0 on his way to save me. I was going to have to be strong, fearless, and ruthless. If I spent too much time wallowing in a sinkhole of regrets, it would swallow me whole too.

A soft ding came over the public address system, indicating it was time for me to return to my seat. The soothing voice of the pilot indicated our descent into LA had begun. My old life was over. My new life was about to begin.

EIGHT

In an in-law apartment on the bottom level of a midcentury LA home on a hill overlooking Silver Lake that I had booked on Airbnb, I set my suitcases on the floor and admired the funky décor: the retro tulip chairs, the faux-zebra rug, the pistachio-colored kitchen walls. It was nothing like my old house in Florida, with its beige walls, beige floors, beige mentality. Beige was my kryptonite, I resolved.

After I unpacked, I traipsed down a hidden staircase that cut between the California bungalows and Spanish Revival houses to Intelligentsia Coffee on Sunset Boulevard. I waited in line behind a rail-thin blond girl in a trucker hat with a rooster and the word COCK on it and a sullen-faced blue-haired guy in a black T-shirt with a glowering skull on it that I recognized as merch from the punk band the Misfits. Outside, I sipped on my soy chai latte and surveyed the hipster mecca scene. It had been fourteen years since I had lived in LA. Everyone was younger, and I was older. Scraps of conversation drifted through the air: *I'm writing a script, I'm auditioning for a pilot, I'm in a band.* In Southwest Florida, people had different conversations: *I'm retired, I'm heading out to play pickleball, I'm embarking on a cruise.* I had escaped God's waiting room before my name had been called. Now I was living in the City of Angels, where everyone was hustling 24/7, no one could afford to retire, and who you were was whomever you decided to be on that particular day.

At my rental, I opened my laptop and started searching Craigslist for my own place. Rents had skyrocketed. I had some money from the divorce settlement, but my bank account was going to drain quickly from the cost of living in my home state. Two hours later, dusk had descended. I went in the backyard and sat in the chair swing. In the distance, the downtown skyline sparkled, a crown at the top of its tallest tower. I could feel the numbness inside of me receding, giving way to a sense of excitement. I had traded what had seemed like security for control over my destiny. The risk was greater, but so was the reward. I didn't know what would happen, but it wouldn't look like what I had before: a life in which I was disappearing into the proverbial yellow wallpaper.

The next few days were spent touring apartments. I couldn't afford the ones I liked, and the ones I could afford had peeling paint, rusty water pipes, uneven floors. I gave up and went north up Interstate 5, to the Valley, where rents were lower. In the Valley's southeast corner, on a tree-lined street in a neighborhood called Magnolia Park, in Burbank, I spotted a FOR RENT sign planted at the base of a palm tree in the front yard of a midcentury building. I dialed the phone number on the sign, and half an hour later, I was following the landlord through the gate.

"Florida, huh?" Bob was chatty, Italian, a septuagenarian, his dyed-brown hair tucked under a white golf cap. Before he had gotten into real estate, he informed me, he had worked in the marketing department for Playboy Records. "I bet you're glad to be here! Me? I grew up in New Jersey, but now I'm a California guy. So, let me warn you, Susannah," he continued as we walked past the oval courtyard pool and climbed a flight of concrete stairs to a second-floor unit in the back, "this place is not for everybody. It's *unique.*"

The two-bedroom unit seemed like it hadn't been remodeled since it was built. It had hardwood flooring, a baby-pink vintage stove, a pink tiled bathtub. It was exactly the sort of place my ex, a fan of new construction, acres of travertine, and shiny stainless-steel appliances, would have hated. To me, this place had *character.* It was *perfect.*

"I'll take it," I told him.

A week later, I closed the front door and looked around the space. I had left my ex all the furniture; I hadn't wanted anything in my new life that might remind me of my old one. But I had nowhere to sit or sleep. I spent the week picking out some inexpensive furnishings: a gray sectional sofa, a table-and-chairs set for the breakfast nook, a bed. Compared with when I had been married, I didn't have much, and I was slightly embarrassed by my sparsely decorated apartment. Then again, my freedom was...*priceless.*

Three weeks later, there was a knock at the door. The UPS guy had the boxes I had asked my friend to ship me from Florida. In the living room, I sliced open a random box with a knife. The envelope that contained the letter Jack had written me years ago sat on top. I removed the contents. I sat on the floor and read a xeroxed copy of a 1984 news article from the *Monitor*, a magazine I had never heard of and which, I would learn, was published by the American Psychological Association, titled "The Triumph and Tragedy of Longitudinal Work."

On the first page, there was a photo of Jack at his paper-covered desk in Tolman Hall. He was staring at the camera, his gaze steely. His erect pose suggested a man of imperturbable confidence. His left hand was resting on the arm of his chair, his elbow cocked as if he might at any moment jump up; his right hand was on his desk, holding his eyeglasses. On a corkboard behind him, there was a photo of Jeanne, smiling. She had died three years before.

According to Jack, conducting a longitudinal study was like "putting an albatross on your back, mounting the back of a tiger and grabbing a bear by the tail all at the same time." As the data from one set of assessments arrived, he had to prepare for the next series of assessments. Funding had to be secured. Scientific papers had to be written. By this point, we, the cohort, were in our teens. We had been generating data that had to be reviewed, analyzed, and cataloged for well over a decade. And the study had only just reached its midway point. "This thing has a beginning," he rued to the reporter, "but it has no end."

Clearly, Jack was brokenhearted by the loss of Jeanne,

his partner and close collaborator. It seemed as though his commitment to their project after her death was an act of devotion, a symbol of his undying love for her. I set the article aside and went in the bedroom. Out the horizontal window I could see the Verdugo Mountains were cast in a lavender glow from the setting sun. There was a bigger story here, I could see now: about love and what a person would do to protect it, people and the ties that bind them, the loyalty that forges those unions, and the lengths we will go to in order to make those connections last a lifetime.

A few days later, I decided it was time to call my mother. I hadn't spoken with her since I'd seen her in Berkeley, two years before. It was hard to be around her, to feel like she wished I didn't exist; it made me feel like *I* wished I didn't exist. But if I told her I got divorced maybe she could relate to that, be empathetic. I dialed her number. She was happy to hear from me, but when I told her that my marriage had ended, she didn't say much. Maybe she thought I was dumb for marrying someone even though she had warned me against it, or maybe my divorce reminded her of my father leaving her. I got off the phone, feeling more alone than I had before. As I sat on the sofa, I put my head in my hands. If I no longer existed, would that make her happy? *Maybe it would be a good idea if I didn't talk to her for a while,* I decided.

I knew I couldn't dwell on the situation with my mother. I had a more pressing issue to address: money. I had the settlement from the divorce, but that was it. Since I had spent my career as a freelancer, I didn't have a 401(k), or a pension, or anything approximating a retirement plan. The divorce money *was* my retirement money. And I wasn't going to touch that.

I had to find a job—part-time, full-time, so long as money was coming in, it didn't matter. I had walked out of my marriage and fallen off a financial cliff. According to a study from the US Government Accountability Office I had seen on the news, women in my age bracket who got divorced saw an income drop of 41 percent. Some mornings I jerked awake from a nightmare in which I was free-falling, plummeting into a bottomless abyss.

Day after day, I submitted résumé after résumé, applying for any role that had to do with words, no matter how remotely: editing, writing, blogging, copywriting, marketing. I reached out to friends and former co-workers, like the dispensers of career advice advised, but even promising leads fizzled. Over the next few months, I sent out in the neighborhood of two hundred résumés. Out of those résumés, I scored a dozen or so interviews. Out of those interviews, I received no job offers. I was overqualified or underqualified, too experienced or didn't have enough relevant experience, wasn't what they were looking for or was told they were pursuing other candidates. The balance in my bank account declined in a mirror image of my self-confidence.

Getting divorced was a mistake, I couldn't help but think, as I soaked in a tub of lukewarm water. The tub was so small the only way I could lie down in it was to prop up my legs on the opposite wall. (*Were people shorter in the 1950s?* I brooded.) Then I remembered how unhappy I had been. This was better than that. Anything was better than that.

One day I took a break from my job search to check my email, and there was a message from an editor I had worked for before. He wanted to know if I would be interested in editing a new section of their website. The subject was right up my alley, he explained: vice. As the section editor, he told me over the phone, I would recruit new writers who would write about everything from alcohol to guns to cannabis to sex. I would cover the vice beat as a contributor. It was a part-time, independent contractor job, with no benefits, and the pay wasn't enough to cover my expenses, but it was a start. I accepted on the spot.

I hung up the phone, collapsed onto the sofa, and breathed a sigh of relief. The job would start in a few weeks. I had one task I wanted to do before that. On my laptop, I clicked over to a webpage I had bookmarked. During my job search, I had come across what seemed like a way I could fund my Block Project story. As a long-time freelancer, I knew I would probably have to juggle more than one gig to pay my bills. This was a way to do that.

At UC Berkeley, the Investigative Reporting Program, or IRP—an independent newsroom and "teaching hospital" where graduate students in journalism got hands-on experience with investigative reporting—was offering three fellowship positions to investigative journalists working on independent projects. The role provided a salary, benefits, and support. If I got one, I could research my story in the same place my story had begun.

"I applied for the Berkeley fellowship, but I'm sure I won't get it," I told Sara, a writer friend, when we met for lunch at a popular Mediterranean restaurant in Atwater Village. "I'm not an investigative journalist the way they mean it." In my mind, an investigative journalist was a guy who wore a fedora with an ID card in the band that read PRESS, spent his days filing Freedom of Information Act requests, and was very, very serious. I wrote about sex and porn and vice. I was neither Woodward nor Bernstein. Years ago, I had written a regular sex column for a website called Beer.com. For a year and a half, I had made a hundred dollars an hour as a freelance copywriter for Procter & Gamble, writing copy for Pepto Bismol on social media. I had a talent for impersonating a bottle of pink bismuth, not speaking truth to power. The fellowship deciders would see right through my bullshit and disqualify me.

"Why? Why not you? Why some *guy*?" Sara said, waving her hands. She was wild-eyed, wild-haired, a wild woman who suffered no fools. "They would be lucky to have you. You are *great* at this. You are *so* good at this."

At the next table, a woman shoveled a spoonful of hummus into the gaping mouth of her towheaded baby daughter. Abruptly, the girl vomited, a river of hummus spilling down her front. As the mother cleaned up the mess, I thought of the tumor baby. It would be five now. In kindergarten. I wondered if its adoptive parents had sent it to a kindergarten for regular kids or a special kindergarten for tumor babies. Were it the former, the other kids might beat it up or ask it why it looked the way it did or kick it violently as if it were a ball. Were it the latter, it might be able to make friends with the other tumors, recite the alphabet in unison, trade snacks at lunch, have playdates at other tumor babies' houses.

The mother resumed inserting hummus into her daughter's mouth. Possibly a part of the mother would always want what I had—no kids, no partner, no one to answer to but myself—and a part of me would always want what the mother had—a child, a partner (I assumed, seeing the diamond ring on her finger), a family. Seemingly, you couldn't have it all, but not because that was the way the game had been rigged, or because you were a woman, but because there was something about being human, no matter your gender or non-binary identity, that made you long for what you didn't have, to want to escape yourself, to be the Other.

It was springtime when an email from the IRP appeared in my inbox. I had scored an interview for one of the prestigious fellowships. It was mine to lose.

––––––

The IRP was housed in a pale brick building across the street from the north side of the UC Berkeley campus, underscoring its affiliation with and separation from the university itself. On the corner of Hearst and Euclid, I ducked into the warmth of the bustling café. The north side was my old stomping grounds. When I was a kid, my parents took us for pizza at the restaurant up the street. When I was a teen, my girlfriends and I hung out after dark in the parking lot down the street, smoking clove cigarettes and pretending we were badasses. When I was an undergrad, my father and I met for lunch at this very café.

A few minutes before eleven, I walked into the IRP. At the front desk, I waited for someone to appear. A cabinet was filled with some of the many journalism awards that Lowell Bergman, who had founded the IRP in 2007, had won, among them a Pulitzer, an Emmy, a Polk, and a Peabody. I didn't have a cabinet of journalism awards at home because I hadn't won any. My longform story about the Great Recession's impact on the porn business was widely read, shared, and acclaimed, but the powers that be in investigative journalism weren't in the business of handing out awards for Best Exposé of the Sex Business. In a framed photo, a beaming Bergman chummed around with Russell Crowe and Al Pacino, who had played a character inspired by Bergman in Michael Mann's Academy Award–nominated 1999 movie *The Insider*. To prepare for my interview, I had talked to a woman who had worked at the IRP for several years. *It's a boys' club*, she had confided after a lot of prodding.

Ten minutes later, I was escorted into the meeting room, where Bergman and his right-hand man at the IRP, John Temple, were sitting.

"Hi, I'm Susannah," I said, extending my hand.

After the two men greeted me, they went back to discussing a documentary they were producing about a spate of deadly military helicopter crashes. I dug around in my bag for a notepad and pen in case I had to take notes during the interview. I scribbled something down so I looked like I was doing something. As I busied myself with looking busy, it occurred to me that I might have had better luck being awarded a big deal academic fellowship if I were working on a story of greater importance, one that exposed government corruption, concerned itself with Trump and Russia, or fingered corporate abuses—not a totally personal tale of my tenure as a human guinea pig. I examined the lines on my palms. I suppressed an urge to leave. Unfortunately, it was too late to escape, seeing as I was here already.

"Sorry I'm late!" Geeta Anand dashed into the room. A new professor at the Graduate School of Journalism, the Mumbai, India–born journalist had won a Pulitzer as a *Wall Street Journal* reporter, and a story she had written about a father who had cofounded a biotechnology company to develop a drug that would save two of his children from a deadly disease had inspired a movie starring Harrison Ford.

Thank god, I thought. *I'm not the only woman here.*

"So," Temple, who had gray hair and the stooped shoulders of a middle-aged beta male, began. He studied the paper on the table in front of him as if he was about to deliver an important monologue. He looked up at me and asked incredulously: "Why should we pick *you* for this fellowship?"

Why *should* they pick me? That was a good question. Perhaps I had made a terrible mistake, believing (or hoping) that my writing career might be viewed as something approximating that of a real investigative journalist, which these folks so obviously were. I was a phony, a fraud, a fake, I thought, consumed by the same self-doubts Jeanne and Gjerde had described seeing in the cohort's girls and young women. *You shouldn't pick me,* I wanted to tell him. *I am a very bad choice. In all likelihood, I will fuck this up.*

Temple was waiting, watching me. Bergman shifted in his seat, bored by the absence of anything interesting happening. Anand looked on expectantly.

"Because my story isn't like any other story," I replied.

"I don't have time to help, okay," Bergman interjected.

Good to know, I thought. *I don't need a fucking babysitter.*

"I mean, have you done reporting like this before? Real, actual investigative reporting?" Temple's expression was one of dubiousness.

The feeling that I was an imposter was now gone, having been replaced by a desire to punch him square in the nose.

"This isn't the type of story we usually do here," Bergman chimed in. "Our investigations drive systemic change. Your story is...*personal*, you could say." He flicked his hand in the air, as if shooing away an annoying fly.

Right, I thought. *Because from your ancient, outdated, patriarchal point of view, a woman's story is personal, and a man's story is important.*

"Great," I said. "It'll be an experiment."

Afterward, I walked back to my rental car, feeling humiliated. I had wasted my time and money on an interview that would lead nowhere, like all the other job interviews I'd had. My overactive imagination had led me to believe I had a chance. Bergman and Temple had disabused me of that notion. This was a sign that I should give up my quest, find a real job, write about something else.

I drove around town and ended up parked in front of the house where I had grown up in the hills. The new owners had painted the house's exterior a pleasing cream color and planted the front yard with drought-tolerant plants: agave, blue-eyed grass, purple sage. I debated whether or not to knock on the front door, ask if I could see my old bedroom, find out if the magnolia tree in the backyard was still blooming, request permission to strip away some of the paint on the doorframe between the kitchen and the hallway so I could see where our parents had charted the growth of my sister and me over the years with a pencil. But I didn't.

I was back in LA when the email from the IRP arrived several weeks later. Could I call their office please? the operations guy wanted to know.

"We would like to offer you one of the fellowships!"

Are you fucking kidding me? I wanted to ask him.

"That's fantastic," I heard myself saying.

If I wanted the fellowship, I would have to move back to the Bay Area for the duration of the fellowship. Over two decades had passed since I had last lived in the Bay Area, and the idea of moving back to Berkeley was about as appealing to me as the prospect of sticking my hand in my kitchen sink's garbage disposal while it was running. But this was too good an opportunity to pass up. I set aside my ambivalence and took the fellowship. It started in the fall.

In the meantime, I preoccupied myself with work. Since the recreational use of cannabis had been legalized in California in 2016, I went to a cannabis dispensary in North Hollywood, the city just west of Burbank, bought a $40 THC-laced candy bar for a story about high-end cannabis products, went home, popped a chocolate cube into my mouth, and waited for something to happen. An hour later, my neck pain had disappeared, but I had also convinced myself I had forgotten how to swallow and had a panic attack. I tossed the weed bar in the trash.

When Paul Manafort, Donald Trump's 2016 presidential campaign manager, went on trial for tax fraud, bank fraud, and failing to disclose a foreign bank account in Virginia, I wrote about a $15,000 ostrich-leather jacket cited by the prosecution as an example of Manafort's extravagant spending habits. I called a few luxury men's clothing stores on Rodeo Drive to figure out where he might have purchased such a garment. A friendly salesperson at one boutique related that while they did not have any ostrich-leather jackets they could offer me an alligator-leather jacket for $85,000. I declined.

In the loft of a tech start-up in the downtown arts district, I donned a virtual reality headset to test out virtual reality porn. At one point, the virtual penis of the virtual male star of the virtual sex scene I was viewing detached from his virtual body. It was a bug in the software that the developer referred to as "a phantom-limb penis syndrome."

It occurred to me that if I was writing about sex (among other things), I should be having it, too. Over the course of my marriage, the ex and I had had sex less and less. (The irony of a sex writer married to a man who did not want to have sex with her had not escaped me.) Looking to make up for lost time, I downloaded several dating apps and started swiping. I met my first date, The Pilot, at a sushi restaurant. He was cute but not super hot, nice but somewhat boring, a smart guy who seemed like a safe bet. Since marrying someone who was "never, ever boring" had gotten me into trouble, I tried to overlook this one's boring parts. The breaking point came after our second date.

"Your dick is broken?" I asked as we lay in my bed.

"No," he went back to trying to explain, sounding flustered. "It happened a year ago. I was dating this woman, and she was, um, on top, and there was this popping noise." He trailed off. "There's scar tissue. It's bent." He sighed.

Of all the penises in all the towns in all the world, I get the broken one. I gave it my best shot, but it was like trying to have sex with a crowbar.

The Attorney and I went to a fancy Italian restaurant. He drove a Range Rover and wore bespoke suits. After dinner, he took me to his home, a beautiful midcentury-modern house in the trees. In the backyard, we walked down a stone path to his swimming pool.

"I'm going for a swim," I announced as we stood next to the pool. I kicked off my heels, stripped off my top, peeled off my jeans, and unfastened my bra. In my black lace thong, I slipped underwater. I floated on my back. The stars twinkled in the night sky. *I could live like this*, I thought. By the next morning I had sobered up and realized over breakfast that I was more interested in the house than I was in his personality.

In late summer, I went out with The Producer of a long-running reality television dating and relationship series. We had drinks at a loud bar on the west side. At his tidy Brentwood condo, he explained earnestly that while he didn't like having sex, per se, he was interested in eating my ass. I thanked him for the offer and passed.

I was careful to make sure none of the guys I went out with had a chance to break up with me. Instead, I ghosted them before they could ghost me. This time, I was the one who was in control. My heart was bruised and broken from my marriage, and I wasn't going to let that happen again. So I became the ghost, hard to see and even harder to grasp.

At the end of August, I put my furniture in a storage unit, packed several boxes of stuff and my suitcases into my car, and headed north. Sight unseen, I had rented a North Berkeley Hills basement apartment in a cozy house occupied by a warm and friendly family. For the next year, I would be living less than a mile from the house in which I had been raised.

Almost six hours later, I drove into the Bay Area. Over the past two decades, technology had transformed the landscape, from the San Francisco skyline to Silicon Valley. On a January day in 1967, Timothy Leary had called upon the tens of thousands of hippies who had gathered in Golden Gate Park for the Human Be-In event to "Turn on, tune in, drop out." Now tech bros in Patagonia vests who ran start-ups had descended like a swarm of Tesla-driving locusts. In San Francisco, the phallic Salesforce Tower dwarfed the Transamerica Pyramid. In Menlo Park, down the peninsula, Facebook had erected a panopticon from which it could see everything but into which few could see. As I entered Berkeley, I noticed the surveillance cameras at the intersections. An app on my mobile phone was busy data mining my route. Everywhere I went, Big Brother was watching me.

That night, I unpacked and settled in to my new place. My apartment had a small kitchen, a low-ceilinged bathroom, a deck that was my own. It felt comfortable and safe. By the time I finished, the sun was setting. I went out on the deck and climbed on a bench. From where I stood, I could see from the hills to the flatlands to the Bay itself. Past the span of the Golden Gate Bridge, the sky was a riot of tangerine, fuchsia, and gold rays.

NINE

On my first morning at the IRP, I set up my belongings on a desk in the cubicle space that I shared with the two other academic fellows, both women, documentary filmmakers who were out of the office working on their projects. The open–floor-plan space was abuzz with the sounds of editors and journalists at work. I opened my laptop computer and created a new Word file. It was hard to think with all of the other keyboards clacking. I was used to writing by myself without these distractions. Hours later, I had generated nothing.

I got up, walked out of the IRP, and crossed the street. Moments later, I was heading down a shaded tree-lined path. Shortly thereafter, I turned onto a sloping tributary path that cut between the trees. At the bottom of the slope, I crossed a wood bridge over a bubbling stream. On the other side, I climbed up a flight of stone steps embedded in the hillside among outcroppings of green growth. At the top, I stepped back into the sunlight.

From the top of a hill, I could see Tolman Hall, where we had been assessed for years after we had finished preschool. Constructed in 1962, the hulking cast-in-place concrete structure had been designed by the Bay Area architect Gardner Dailey, a pioneer of the Second Bay Tradition. The building had been named for Edward C. Tolman, a UC Berkeley psychology professor who had studied rats in mazes and coined the term "cognitive map."

I started down the hill and circumnavigated the building on its south side. Inside, I knew, the structure was famously labyrinthine; professors and students alike got lost in its complex of corridors. When I reached the entrance to the west tower, I stopped. The building was empty, as silent as a mausoleum. I had read that it was going to be torn down and replaced with a newer, shinier building. I opened one of the metal and glass doors and stepped into the lobby.

To my left, some of the letters over the doorway were missing.

N   ITUTE
O F
H U   N   DE   L   PMENT

This was the way to the Institute of Human Development, or IHD, which had overseen the Child Study Center when I had attended it. I walked through the opening. In the vestibule, the phone booths were stripped of their equipment. I went up the stairs. As I walked down the hall, I saw that some of the push-button office door locks had been ripped from their moorings with a crowbar. At the end of the hall, I turned right. Near the end of that hall, I found a door with a sign that warned: ADMITTANCE WITH PERMISSION ONLY. I opened the door.

Inside there was a long, narrow observation room. On the left side, a row of one-way mirrors and a built-in desk faced an experiment room. I walked out of the observation room and around the corner to the experiment room. The door was decorated with kid-friendly images: a rabbit in a carrot car, a donkey and a leopard in a hot-air balloon, a cow in a bassinet. In the experiment room, I attempted to see the observation room from which the researchers would have been spying into this room, but the only thing I could see was my own reflection.

I kept going. There were more observation rooms and experiment rooms. There were psychology manuals, wall charts, notebooks. There was a room labeled THE BABY LAB, the walls of which were yellow and turquoise and in which a pink-framed one-way mirror was lower because the subjects had been smaller. Eventually, I lost my sense of direction. This was how Tolman's rats felt, I thought, scurrying through his mazes in search of some cheese.

Upstairs, there were more observation rooms and experiment rooms. In a pale-blue room with a brown dog, a yellow cat, a green turtle, a blue squirrel holding an acorn, and a red bird painted on the walls, there were surveillance cameras concealed in screened boxes in the corners where the walls met the ceiling. In the adjoining observation room, the controller enabled the observer-operator to ZOOM, FOCUS, or adjust the IRIS of the cameras. In the department office, the mailboxes had been emptied, and the door had been pulled from its hinges.

After a while, I walked into an experiment room on the south side of the building. *This is where I got left with the M&M's; this is where I realized there was someone behind the mirror,* I realized. In my memory, the room was bigger. But the room wasn't smaller. *I* was bigger. It was like the scene in *Alice's Adventures in Wonderland* when Alice eats the cake marked EAT ME and grows telescopically to nine feet tall. The one-way mirror was broken. Shards of mirror were strewn across the carpet. In the shattered mirror, my reflection was in pieces.

When I emerged from Tolman Hall, the sun had sunk lower in the sky, and the shadows had grown longer. I checked my phone. I had been in there for hours. I headed up the hill to the IRP, thinking about how it seemed as if the past and the present were overlapping.

———

Every weekday, and often on the weekends, I went to the IRP, where I worked on my story. It didn't matter if the space was crowded and noisy or empty and quiet. I kept struggling with the writing. I wrote words, lots some days. Then I reread them. Then I deleted them. The words were the wrong ones or that's how it seemed. I didn't get what the story was about or how to tell it or that's how it felt. I was intimidated by the subject matter, even though I, myself, had been a subject in the Block Project. I couldn't stop feeling like I was an imposter who had faked her way into a fellowship she didn't deserve. So I kept doing more research, figuring that if I immersed myself into the story, I might be able to find my way out of it.

Before we were studied at Tolman Hall, we were studied at the Child Study Center. When I had last visited Berkeley, I had gotten a tour of the preschool. One afternoon a few months after I had moved back to Berkeley for the fellowship, I returned to the preschool. In the observation gallery overlooking the east-side play yard, I peered through the sheet of Mylar hung in front of the screened-in frame. In the play yard, twenty or so preschoolers and their teachers had formed a loose half circle. Many of the children were in costume, even though it wasn't Halloween: two Batmans, a Chewbacca, a *Tyrannosaurus Rex*, a cat, a soccer player, an Elsa from *Frozen*, and a fireman. Most of the kids were sitting on the ground, some were standing, and a few were either meandering about in a state of bored distraction or were preoccupied with whatever else had garnered their attention. At the front of the group, a Berkeley Police Department patrol officer was delivering a stern lecture on stranger danger.

"Is it a *kid*'s job to help an *adult*?" the officer queried.

"No!" the children screamed in unison.

"It's another *adult*," the officer agreed, nodding his head thoughtfully. "What do you do if any adult tries to *grab* you?"

"Run away!" a boy yelled.

"Tell somebody!" a girl offered.

"That's *right*," the officer said, pleased.

Prior to entering the observation gallery, I had been

cautioned not to make any noise that might reveal to the children that someone was watching them. PLEASE MAINTAIN **COMPLETE SILENCE** WHEN OBSERVING IN THE GALLERY, a sign reminded me in case I forgot and started talking to myself. Careful not to make a sound, I turned the page in my notebook, which I had situated on the same built-in desk where a Block Project researcher had taken notes on me as he or she had sat on the same blue-topped metal stool upon which I was sitting. These days, the cramped gallery was doing double duty as a storage closet. I sat amid child things: a chalkboard easel, milk crates of plastic dinosaurs and wooden blocks, pink doll-size strollers, a bin of ratty stuffed animals.

The officer concluded his presentation, and the children scattered like chickens. The yard buzzed with the serious business of child's play: A trio of boys raced their tricycles back and forth in front of the gallery, shouting directions and careening wildly; the fireman and one of the Batmans assembled a tower out of plastic blocks; a girl thrust her hands into the raised sandbox as she muttered to herself. Eventually, the teacher announced it was naptime, and the children migrated toward the east classroom, where, I had seen, neat rows of small cots had been outfitted with the blankets and toys they required to rest or sleep. As I gathered my things, the door to the play yard at the south end of the gallery opened. Sunlight poured in.

A teacher hefted in a tricycle. A blond girl wearing a gray dress decorated with stars and Mary Janes coated in pink glitter peered into the gallery from behind the teacher's skirt and spotted me. Her blue eyes widened. Her mouth formed a tiny O of surprise. Accidentally, the teacher had exposed me in my hiding place. Unsure what to do, I smiled and waved. Hurriedly, the teacher shut the door, but it was too late. The girl had seen me. As I left the gallery, I wondered if the girl would spend the rest of her life thinking behind every closed door someone—or something—was watching her, or if the memory would be lost to time.

In the preschool's administration building, a woman led me on a tour of the experiment rooms where we had been assessed one-on-one by researchers, the same rooms where I had remembered being taken, that I had been told were game rooms, in which I had played with toys and been given gifts. The one-way mirrors and eavesdropping equipment were still there, but some experiment rooms had been converted into offices. Since the late 1990s, state funding of the UC system had shrunk, the woman explained. As a result, UC Berkeley struggled with a lack of space. The preschool was no exception.

"We have boxes of a few things in a closet that might be of interest to you," the woman said as I followed her down the hall. I waited in a meeting room decorated with art by the students. She returned with the boxes and left me to go through them.

Digging through the first box, I realized its materials were related to research that had predated the Block Project: the Inter-Generational Studies (IGS). The IGS had comprised three longitudinal studies—the Guidance Study, the Berkeley Growth Study, and the Oakland

Growth Study. Launched in 1928 by Jean Walker Macfarlane, a psychology professor and the IHD's founder, the Guidance Study had been a lifelong survey of human development. It had begun with a cohort of 250 Berkeley newborns and had grown to include their children and in some cases their grandchildren. The Blocks had analyzed that dataset for insight into adolescent personality development, a formative experience that had laid the groundwork for the Block Project.

From the contents, I extracted a stack of black-and-white photos. I spread them out across the table. This was one of the IGS cohorts. The photos had been overlaid with tracing paper, the outlines of the subjects traced and annotated with their code numbers in their study. These were the ghosts of my human lab rat ancestors. Flipping through the guest book from a 1985 reunion of the cohort, I realized I wasn't the only one whose life had been impacted by being studied. "What wonderful memories we all have," one subject had written. "You have been a real part of my life," another had opined. "You were interested in me when I needed someone & it has continued, Bless you," another had enthused. "You always made me feel I was worth a lot. You still do!" one had gushed. One of the notes had been addressed, fondly, "To Our Study Mother."

So it wasn't just me, I thought. *It was them too.*

PROF BLOCK FILES SAVE! had been scrawled across the top of the next box. It held files from the Block Project. I scanned the file tabs for hints to their contents: Divorce Questionnaire, Relationship of Parental Teaching Strategies to Ego-Resiliency, Instruction for the Parent/Child

Interaction Tasks, Master: Physionomic [*sic*] Perceptions, Blank Interview Forms, Phenomenology of Emotion.

There were drawings, protocols, and scripts for our assessments. For one test, we were given a puzzle to assemble. "Give enough help so that C"—the "C" represented us: the Child—"is not frustrated as he works on the Puzzle," the instructions advised. But there was a trick: The pieces of the puzzle didn't fit together. Of course, they didn't tell us the puzzle wasn't solvable. "When C says that the pieces will not fit, E"—the "E" represented them: the Examiner—"should act puzzled but should refrain from asking questions or making assumptions that might encourage hypothesis formation." What were they trying to assess? How long we could work on a puzzle designed to frustrate us before throwing it against the wall? "Let C work on barrier piece for 15 seconds without responding to his verbalizations if at all possible. When a response is demanded, reflect, 'The piece won't fit?' (quizzically)." The test was terminated when "(1) C is no longer actively engaged in problem solving or (2) C moves the piece about mindlessly in such a way that it is clear he is no longer trying to solve the problem." It seemed like a commentary on my larger investigation of the study itself. Even now I wasn't sure how all the pieces fit together or if they did.

In the next box, there were small envelopes with familiar green plastic triangle pieces, numbered purple wooden connector rods, and laminated printed cards bound with rubber bands. Our parents were instructed to sort the cards into categories ranging from least descriptive to most descriptive of their parenting styles. "When

I am angry with my child, I let him know it," one read. "I don't want my child to be looked upon as different from others," another read. "I expect a great deal of my child," yet another read.

I picked up a sheet. "Resistance to Temptation" was the name of this test. It took place in a "small experimental room" in which there was a set of "attractive toys"—a Sasha doll, a dollhouse, a tow truck—on a table and a set of "unattractive, old toys"—a comb, a broken car, "a small, bent, green plastic tree"—on the floor. We were told the "attractive toys" belonged to "a lady who is playing some different games with children and we can't play with them." Then the examiner pretended to have forgotten something and left the room. On the other side of the one-way mirror, the examiner started a stopwatch. "AS SOON AS THE CHILD TOUCHES any of the attractive toys, record time and go immediately into the room," the instructions directed. Did I resist temptation? Given that I tackled a bowl of M&M's: unlikely.

The woman appeared in the doorway.

"Do you know if the preschool kept a file on me?"

"Hmm, let me see," she said and went to investigate.

A few minutes later, she reappeared, holding a long and faded index card box. *Please*, I thought, as she flipped through the decades-old cards.

"There you are," she said.

She handed me the card.

At the top of the card, there was a number over my name: 1685. That was the preschool's number for me. If— and this was a big if, because so many years had passed—the university still had the preschool's original file on me, that number was the key to finding it.

———

At the IRP, I logged onto the UC Berkeley Library website. If I found my file from the preschool, perhaps that could lead me to the file that the Block Project had maintained on me. At the top of the webpage, I entered *Harold E. Jones Child Study Center* into the search bar. I clicked the button, hoping for something. "Yes," I said, pumping my fist twice in the air. There was more than something. At the university's offsite storage facility, there were sixty-three boxes that contained the Child Study Center records from 1927 to approximately 1980. That was thirty-nine linear feet. Their contents included "children's development files, photographs, and reports." I could explain to someone at the library why I needed to look in the boxes of records, that personal information might be contained in there somewhere, and get permission to dig through them in search of my file. It would be like trying to find a needle in a haystack, only the needle was my file and the haystack was the preschool archive.

"You can't look at those, that's not how this works." The librarian, who had a solemn expression and curly short hair, shook her head vigorously. This was the self-appointed protector of the archives, I surmised. Through the library website, I had been able to identify the boxes most likely to contain my preschool file: Box 19, Box 20, and Box 21. In the hope of expediting the process, I had walked from the IRP to the library on campus. But the librarian stood squarely in the way. "There are privacy issues," she said from behind her desk. A research librarian would have to search for my file, if there was one, in the boxes. And if that person did find my file, I would have to get permission from someone else to view it. "You need permission to see your file. A letter from the director of the Institute of Human Development. That is *required*."

A few weeks later, I had secured the letter from the IHD's director. Online I submitted the letter with an application for "Access to Restricted Materials." Several weeks passed. I checked and rechecked my email. I was starting to wonder if I would ever find my preschool file when an email from the library landed in my inbox. My preschool file was at the library. I grabbed my stuff and headed over.

At the Bancroft Library, which contain UC Berkeley's special collections, I waited at the front desk of the Heller Reading Room as the librarian retrieved the file. At rows of desks under the barrel ceiling, students and researchers were studying their materials. The librarian appeared, file in hand.

"You can't take it out of the room." She frowned. "You can't make copies of it. You *can* take photos of it. And you have to wear these." She handed me a pair of white gloves.

I sat down at a long desk in the back of the room. Outside the north-facing windows, students on the expansive, gently sloping lawn were tossing a Frisbee, eating their lunches, taking a nap. I opened the file.

The first page was titled "Nursery School Entrance Form." Right away, I recognized the handwriting as my mother's. This was information she had shared with the preschool after I had been accepted and had begun attending. For my father's special interests, she had written: "Basketball (plays)"; for hers, she had written: "piano"; and for the family's special interests, she had written: "Beaches, hiking in Tilden." Tilden was the nearby regional park.

The next page listed my pediatrician's name, my dentist's name, and the dates of my vaccinations. My present state of health, my mother wrote, was "excellent." My birth "normal." I sucked my thumb. I slept with a night-light and a special blanket. I had to be "urged to eat." Strangely, I disliked "chocolate, cake, and soda." (*What kind of kid doesn't like chocolate, cake, and soda?*) I was potty-trained by eighteen months. ("Trained herself," my mother reported.) The preschool had inquired as to what words I used for bathroom activities (so they could use the same words in case any confusion arose, I assumed). "When asked," my mother confided, "Susannah said: Pooh pooh, doo doo, shit and dirty plops." Instructed to select from a set of words the ones she associated with me, my mother circled: "rather inactive," "solitary," and "fairly self sufficient." (I was a lazy, independent loner; duly noted.) My most attractive characteristic was, she shared: "Her interest—close attention—she'll examine a bug or leaf for a long time. She's very eager to learn and will endure quite a lot of frustration, keep on trying to do something, new & difficult." *And how*, I thought. "For example, the 1st day at this school spent ½ hour each exploring the possibility of two new kinds of equipment: a set of nuts and bolts on a wood board, and an array of magnets."

Even then, words were important to me. "She wants to <u>write</u> and <u>read</u> very much, sounds words to read them, writes words & sentences with spelling help," she explained. As for what my father's take on me was, that wasn't included. In the early 1970s, the mother was the expert on the child—supposedly.

The preschooler me wasn't so different from the adult me. I was still solitary, still self-sufficient. Words were still important to me—perhaps too important. And that part about my paying close attention, that was my superpower in journalism, my ability to study someone and get a read on the person. Maybe the Blocks hadn't needed to conduct a thirty-year study of me to figure out who I was going to grow up to be. Maybe the answer was: *She will grow up to be the exact same person.*

I turned the page to find a Wechsler Preschool and Primary Scale of Intelligence test. At four, my IQ was 125. That was higher than I expected, but I was no genius. I was "a lovely child, calm and comfortable tho shy," a note read. On the following pages there were a series of mazes. Maze after maze, I drew a wavering pencil line from the baby chick at one end of the maze to the mother hen at the other end. The last maze, the hardest one, had an "X" in the middle of it and no chickens. I tried to find my way out, but I got lost. The pencil line stopped midway through.

The last page was the original one-page application to the Child Study Center that my parents had submitted. This was the document that had started it all. "Please note filing an application does not ensure a child's enrollment later," the form cautioned any overly optimistic parents. "There are always many more applications for each semester than there are vacancies." At the bottom, it read: "I am interested in participating in research studies of infants and young children conducted through the Child Study Center." Next to the "Yes," my mother had drawn a careful X. The form was stamped May 20, 1968. "Age when app. rec'd," it noted: "1 mo 10 days."

According to this document, my father hadn't left my mother and me in a hospital room on the day I was born to deliver my application to the preschool. Who had told me that story? My mother? My father? Or had I made it up to convince myself I was special? I didn't know. I couldn't trust my own answer. My life story, as I knew it, was a fable.

———

I walked across campus to clear my head. Parts of the campus were the same as when I was a student there—Sather Gate, Wheeler Hall, Doe Library—but other parts of it were different. There were new buildings made of chrome and steel. On Sproul Plaza, the students weren't fighting for freedom of speech, as they had in 1964. They were recruiting fellow students into their activity groups with VOLDEMORT WENT TO STANFORD T-shirts. The Campanile sounded at the top of the hour, its bells ringing pleasantly through the air. But was it actual bells or a digital recording? I wasn't sure what was real and what wasn't. I heard a whirring from behind me. I whipped around to find a robot, a remotely controlled cooler on wheels, delivering a smoothie to a wanting student, and I leaped to get out of its way.

A few mornings later, I visited Wurster Hall, a Brutalist behemoth designed by three architects, one of whom was Esherick, the Child Study Center's architect. In its Environmental Design Archives, I pored over Esherick's papers, which included documentation related to the conceptualizing, design, and construction of the Child Study Center. There were letters and notes and plans. There were orders for the "transparent mirrors" (for observing the preschoolers undetected), discussions of how high the observation gallery should be ("It is important for observers to see the faces of the children close by"), and a breakdown of the cost to build the preschool ($199,999). In a 1958 letter, the director of the child research institute at the University of Minnesota suggested the Berkeley preschool try "equipping individual children with portable transmitters which could broadcast to a central recording unit the whereabouts of the child and his conversation," adding, "After all, we equip Sputniks and Explorers with such devices. Why not living beings! Shades of *1984*!" This approach was not undertaken for reasons not documented. The idea of a portable transmitter was prescient; today a mobile phone fulfilled a similar purpose, but apps did the geolocating and eavesdropping.

As often as I could, I returned to Tolman Hall, to which I had been given a key so I could come and go as I pleased. Graffiti appeared on the walls. Garbage accumulated in the halls. Blinds went askew. More one-way mirrors were broken. One afternoon, I arrived to discover a group of men in hard hats erecting a chain-link fence around the perimeter.

At the IRP, I retrieved a large scroll I had acquired: Tolman Hall's original blueprints. I unrolled it on the floor and turned the pages. I had overlooked the basement. I peered closer. This floor was different. Amid the experiment and observation rooms, there were rooms marked COLONY, PREP, SURGERY, AUTOCLAVE, and ANIMAL DEM. LABS. (I wasn't sure what the DEM. in ANIMAL DEM. LABS stood for. I wasn't sure I wanted to know.) The basement was where other researchers had conducted studies on animals. A week after that, I visited Tolman Hall for the last time, escorted by a man from building maintenance. In hard hats and reflective vests, we descended into the basement. I moved through the gloom; the place was spooky. There were lab rooms, counters for, say, dissecting animals, abandoned autoclaves. I shivered in the frigid air, wondering if there had been an overlap between the animal studies down here and the studies of us kids in the floors above. In the early 1980s, protests by animal rights groups had led the university to halt animal research in Tolman Hall's basement. Before that, our study and the animal studies would have run concurrently. I knew what it had been like for me to be studied. But what had it been like to be studied if you were an animal?

I found an answer online in "My Descent from the Monkey," a paper written by Nicholas S. Thompson, who had studied monkeys in the "beautifully appointed, windowless basement laboratories of Tolman Hall" in the 1960s as a doctoral candidate in comparative psychology at Cal, and published in *Perspectives in Ethology* in 1976.

"From the horror of those days," he recollected, "I remember almost nothing about simian social organization. I remember the constant battle to keep man, monkey, and environment in their separate places." He recalled the "paraphernalia of sanitation," the fear of being bitten, the self-protection garb. "What is significant about this period is that I came to hate monkeys," he continued. His subjects were "incorrigible prisoners, and I was both warden and sole guard." The experience was so disturbing that he left studying primate social behavior altogether and became an ornithologist.

That night I slipped between the bedcovers and turned off the light. You could secure the required consent forms, follow the rules, and look after the interests of your research subjects, but the underlying problem was the power dynamic. Someone was the studier. Someone was the studied. The former had all the power. And the latter had none.

———————

As I kept poring over documents and visiting departments and talking to people who had known or worked with or been peers of the Blocks, a story began to form. It was not my story, but the story of the study itself; in particular, what had happened to it.

After Jack retired, the Block Project's dataset was moved to UC Santa Cruz, where Per Gjerde and two other UCSC psychology professors would oversee it moving forward. In 1999, our last assessments, at age thirty-two, were conducted, as planned. Then, not long after that, Jack demanded the dataset's return to UC Berkeley. Why? The answer depended on whom you asked. According to one source, Jack worried someone else might get credit for the study that he had created with his late wife and to which he had devoted his life; in his mind, the dataset was *his*. A custody battle ensued over the dataset. The universities' provosts were drawn into the fight. In the end, the dataset was trucked back to Berkeley, where it was put in a storage room known as the Big Pink, so named for its pale-pink walls. Jack had agreed Per Gjerde would have continued access to the dataset so he could work on it, but Jack gave Gjerde access to the dataset once and never again. After that, Jack told people he was working on the dataset, but no one was really sure.

In 2009, Jack returned to Tolman Hall for what would be the final time. In his eighties, he was confined to a wheelchair. He was unable to drive so a man had delivered him there. The reason for Jack's return was simple. The data over which he had dominion had to be moved. The space was needed for a sleep study.

The Big Pink was filled with filing cabinets that contained the various datasets of the studies upon which Jack had worked, including ours. He made little headway. The man who had brought Jack there came to retrieve him. The man rolled Jack to the elevator bay, then left him to ask someone about something. Jack didn't notice the woman at the end of the hall who was staring at him. She wondered how this brilliant lion of a man about whom she had heard so much had become this smaller man, so seemingly broken.

After Jack's death the following year, the Inter-Generational Studies data went to the University of California, Davis, for safekeeping. As for the Block Project dataset, a professor from the University of California, Riverside, reviewed it, pulled a thousand pages to send to the Murray Archive, and left the rest. There was an email discussion about what to do with our individual files: our raw data. Someone decided to call waste management.

Waste management delivered garbage cans with locked lids. A woman stuffed the Block Project files through the slots in the garbage can lids. Then waste management retrieved the filled garbage cans and dropped off more garbage cans to fill. This process repeated itself over the course of several weeks: delivering cans, filling them, taking them away.

As I watched giant orange machines operated by men dismantle Tolman Hall, I thought about all of this, including my own file that had been lost. A part of me had believed the study that had predicted who I would grow up to be had known me better than I had known myself. I had fantasized that by finding my data I would find the real me. The structure was coming apart, its walls falling, the sky taking its place. The machines were like dinosaurs. The noise was grinding gears and whining engines. Like my history, Tolman Hall was no more.

TEN

In the fall, the academic fellowship at UC Berkeley concluded, and I moved back to LA. Someone had rented the unit with the vintage pink stove in the Burbank apartment building where I had lived, so I rented another unit on the other side of the courtyard pool. This unit had the same configuration as the old one, but the vintage stove was yellow and the bedroom window faced the window of a second-floor apartment in the beige concrete building to the west, the blinds of which were always drawn.

I got my furniture that was in storage out of storage and arranged it in the various rooms. I unpacked the suitcases that I had brought to the Bay Area and the boxes that I had retrieved from storage, hung my clothes in the bedroom closet and my coats in the hall closet, and bought groceries that I put in the refrigerator and canned goods that I arranged in neat lines in the kitchen cabinets. In the room I had designated to be my home office, I set up my computer. I configured my printer. I filled a red-and-blue ceramic mug that was handmade and given to me by a Marine Corps combat veteran and ceramics studio manager in UC Berkeley's Department of Art Practice (of which my father had long ago been chair) with pencils and pens. One side of the mug read NEVERTHELESS, SHE PERSISTED and the other side had a rendering of the Virgin Mary with seven swords piercing her heart to represent her seven sorrows.

I thought maybe since I was no longer in my hometown, where I had felt crowded by the specter of my past, but in Los Angeles (County, but still), the home I had chosen, I would be able to write. At last, the story would flow out of me. Sentences would unfurl on the page, fully formed and requiring neither revision nor editing. Pages would manifest, one after the next, in short order, as if by magic, muse, or another type of matter from which prose sprang forth. Instead, I sat at my computer and did what I had done at the other end of the state. I typed words and deleted them. I got nowhere. I was blocked, which struck me as fitting, seeing as the name of the study had foretold my predicament (Block Project | blocked).

I tried numerous techniques to unblock myself. In the hope of better understanding the story's structure, I wrote words that seemed important on note cards and covered a wall with them, like a homicide detective in search of a serial killer. I went for long walks, in the morning or the afternoon or the evening, along the sidewalk or the bike path or the alley, past Halloween decorations (October) or Thanksgiving decorations (November) or Christmas decorations (December). I read essays about writing and writer's block and creativity, wept protractedly and self-pityingly, and wallowed in the tub. Mostly, I regretted that I had pulled back the curtain on my personal history, having not uncovered the Block Project file that had, as I understood it, contained thirty years of raw data on me but having discovered that the story of my life had been tossed out like so much trash.

The New Year came and went. In January, reports emerged of a novel virus in China. By March COVID-19-related news was virtually the only news to which anyone paid attention. Lockdowns commenced. Sheltering in place began. I closed the windows and waited for the inevitable conclusion. The world was coming to an end.

Writing felt unimportant. What was the point? No one would be alive to read what I wrote anyway. I focused my energies on binging Netflix, eating cans of SpaghettiOs, and stockpiling toilet paper. My life established a new rhythm, one that I, an introvert, relished. I didn't have to see anyone. I didn't have to go anywhere. I didn't have to be anyone other than who I was when I was alone. As time passed, it dawned on me that throughout my life I had felt an immense pressure to be someone who impressed other people: a smart girl, or a good wife, or a successful journalist. In the safe cocoon of my apartment, I could be who I wanted to be: my imperfect, weird, creative, imaginative, curious, strange, unique self.

But the world was not coming to an end, or not anytime soon. In April, I resolved to return to writing with a different approach. This time, I would treat my subject matter the same way I had treated my journalism subjects and the same way my researchers had studied me: with a cool, calculated objectivity. It worked. I typed words and did not delete them. Having depersonalized my own relationship to my story, I made progress—small, slow, incremental, but progress nevertheless, seeing as I had persisted. Now I had to solve another related problem. Due to the pandemic, my freelance gigs had dried up. I knew I had enough material to turn my story into a book, and an advance from a publisher would pay for the time it would take me to write it. I put a book proposal together and signed a contract with a literary agent. The agent sent the book proposal to book editors. In June, there was a video meeting with a publisher that was interested in publishing the book I was writing— on one condition. The publisher didn't want the book to be journalistic. They wanted it to be a *memoir*.

A memoir was what I didn't want to write. The memoirs on my shelves were by women who had undertaken soul-searching, and they landed on conclusions of hope and optimism. The books ended with the author learning to love herself, or falling in love with someone, or both, and then living happily ever after. Their pages were covered in words that had a single mission: to share *feelings*. I was not especially good at sharing my feelings. I did not particularly want to share my feelings with the world. I would have rather not had feelings at all, had that been an option. I had been taught as a child that feelings were problems that caused upset to other people (my parents). I had spent my life avoiding, squashing, negating my feelings.

Still, I had come so far. It seemed unwise to give up.

I suppressed an urge to point out I was a *journalist*, not a memoirist, and agreed. When the contract arrived, I signed my name on the signatory line. *I can do this*, I told myself. All I had to do was write it.

———————

So I wrote about all things I had never written about before, what I had thought was in my past but had followed me through the course of my life, the story I had kept under wraps because I had thought it made me seem too vulnerable or like a person who made bad choices or like a little girl who longed for things she had not gotten. I wrote about what I had thought happened on the day I was born, the genesis of the Block Project, and my earliest memories of being studied. I wrote about my parents' divorce, my first depression when I was ten, and my mother's unhappiness. I wrote about the bookish girls, the sluts, and the frat row parties. I wrote about being assessed as a teen, Jeanne's death, and meeting Jack. I wrote about my father's death, my second depression when I was twenty-seven, and the first time I went to a strip club. I wrote about meeting a porn star, visiting the set of a porn movie, and what compelled me to move to LA. I wrote about being a journalist, how Porn Valley was a place where I came alive, and my porn collection. I wrote about the move to New Orleans, the hurricane, and my friend taking me in. I wrote about my estrangement from my father's second family, my mother, and my sister. I wrote about being a waitress, moving to Austin, and moving to Chicago. I wrote about meeting the man I would marry, our elopement, and how he had made me feel safe. I wrote about the tumor, the treatment, and the recovery. I wrote about how the experience of being turned into a human lab rat as a cancer patient led me back to the Block Project, how the study's research enlightened me about me, and my trip to California. I wrote about the man I married not turning out to be the man I thought he was, how he frightened me, and how I scared myself. I wrote about the day our marriage ended, our divorce, and leaving Florida. I wrote about moving back to LA, the fellowship at UC Berkeley, and returning to LA once more. I wrote about learning my raw data in the study had seemingly been destroyed, the realization that I had not been special but a data point, and that I would never really know who a psychological experiment had predicted I would grow up to be, not with any kind of specificity, anyway.

Thunk.

It was 2021, and summertime, my apartment a hot box. I got up from my desk and walked to my front door to retrieve the package the Amazon driver had left on my doorstep. I opened the door to a wall of heat. I scooped up the package, tucked it under my arm, and retreated inside. The strained thrumming of the air conditioner working overtime filled the front room. I sat on my sofa and tore open the plastic envelope. It was Jack's final book: *Personality as an Affect-Processing System: Toward an Integrative Theory.* I had read the book in Florida, but lost it during a move. It had been published in 2002, when Jack's health was declining. According to his theory, personality was a system that adapted to the environment around it. Essentially, you were who you were, but you were shaped by your life experiences too. As far as I could tell, the book had been received with the same *thud* that had heralded the arrival of the book at my front door. The Block Project had been spawned in the late 1960s when the very notion of personality had been in question. By the time Jack's book was published, personality was a given. Today, the Big Five theory is dominant; in this model, five traits (openness to experience, conscientiousness, extraversion—often spelled extroversion— agreeableness, and neuroticism) comprise a taxonomy of personality. The debate is over.

I set the book aside. Personality researchers studied people like primatologists studied monkeys. In their minds, a person was a system to be solved, an equation to be calculated, a container from which to harvest precious data. But the Block Project had only known the part of me that I had shown it. We, the cohort, were more than a dataset. There was something ineffable about a person. You could call it spirit or soul or something else, but it was an intangible force, beyond the reach of even the person who possessed it, too elusive to be extracted and quantified by a researcher who had retreated into an ivory tower. That same force was what had propelled me forward, out of the Valley and through the hurricane, past cancer and away from a man I feared, up the state and back again. It was an indomitable spirit, a primal, essential will to survive, or a faith in something greater than science. And it was *mine*.

As I continued to write over the months that followed, a thought began to worry me. A story has three acts. A decade earlier, I had embarked on a hero's journey, in search of a new understanding of myself, the world, and my past. Along the way, I had overcome obstacles, vanquished enemies, and returned home. But in the third act, I was supposed to be transformed. I would fall in love again or learn to love and accept myself in some way I had not previously or release my past to become the person I was always meant to be. But I didn't know if I *had* changed, or if I was the exact same person I had been on the day when, at four, I had stepped cautiously across the threshold of the Child Study Center's west classroom and turned into a human lab rat. I sat at my desk and looked out the window, my computer idle, waiting for something to happen.

My phone rang.

It was mid-June, in 2022, and I had moved to another apartment building not far from the one in which I had been living. At my old apartment, I had lived in a unit over the building manager's unit. During the pandemic, he had developed a habit of smoking weed day and night. I did not mind that he was smoking weed, which was legal in California, only that he was doing it in our nonsmoking building. My clothes and bedding and towels reeking of weed was the problem. Despite my best efforts, I could not get the landlord to make the building manager stop this—he was the building manager, after all, the guy who unclogged our sinks and stopped our toilets from running, so he took precedence over me—so I had moved out.

In the living room of my new apartment, which was in a smaller building, better maintained, and more private, I checked my phone. The call originated from a city in Idaho, a city where, as far as I knew, I knew no one. Typically, when I got a call from a number I didn't recognize on my phone, I let it go to voicemail, assuming it was spam. For some reason, I didn't do that. Instead, I answered the call. It was my sister.

"Mom died this morning," she said. I hadn't spoken to my sister in over a decade, and I hadn't spoken to my mother in five years, hadn't seen her in seven. Countless times, I had imagined getting this call. *Mom is dead,* my sister would say. How would I feel? Would I regret that I had estranged myself from my mother? Would I be overcome with grief? Would I be sorry there was no fixing our relationship, on account of her being dead?

My mother had died of late-stage Alzheimer's, my sister explained. I didn't know my mother had been diagnosed with Alzheimer's. It was awful, my sister continued. My mother had been in and out of the hospital, had lost her mind, had lashed out at those around her, acting crazy. Sometimes she would ask my sister why I wasn't there, and my sister would tell her that I had estranged myself from the family, and after a while my mother would forget what my sister had told her, and my sister would have to tell her all over again. A year and a half ago, my sister had moved from California to Idaho. My mother had remained in California.

As I listened to my sister, I thought about how growing up sometimes we would drive by a rest home on a busy street in Berkeley, and my mother would point to it, and she would remark to my sister and me: *I bet when I'm old you'll leave me there to die!* Then she would laugh, as if she had been joking. But had she been? Perhaps she had suspected that one day one of us would betray her. That because she had so many times said *I don't want to be a mother anymore,* one of us (me, obviously) would come to the conclusion that she (me, that is) didn't want to be her mother's daughter anymore. That hearing that one's own mother, in whose womb one had resided for nine months, did not want you or did not want to parent you (what was the difference, really?), one of us would excuse herself from the relationship, to save herself. Ultimately, my mother had died how she had long feared she would: alone.

My sister told me she would text me with updates about what was to come. In a daze, I hung up the phone, opened the front door, and sat down on the steps. The pine trees cast long shadows across the small courtyard. Nearby, a crow cawed, rattled, and clicked. The scent of freshly cut grass drifted through the air.

How do I feel? The truth was unspeakable. My mother was dead, and the answer was obvious. I was *relieved.* It felt as if a weight had been lifted off me, as if I had been released from an invisible, previously unseen prison, as if, I would tell my friend Sara over lunch, I had been strangled for a very long time, and then the hands around my neck had been released, and I could breathe again, was taking in big gulps of air. My mother was gone; there was no changing that. But I was *alive.* I breathed in, filling my lungs. I breathed out. She would never have to tell me that she did not want to be a mother anymore. Finally, she had found a way out of it.

My sister arranged the memorial service, but I didn't go. The virus was surging, and I didn't want to get sick. But I also wanted to avoid the scene, the laudatory speeches, all the people. I felt guilty about it, but only vaguely, and sent flowers. A few weeks later, I got a text from my sister letting me know the company that had cremated my mother had distributed her cremains, per her wishes. They had been scattered past the Marin Headlands. Bits and pieces of what had been my mother had drifted, floated, descended through the water and past the fishes to the murky depths of the Pacific.

It was late July when I returned from an errand to find an express delivery envelope on my front door mat. Inside, I extracted a copy of my mother's trust. She had left me $50,000, but everything else had gone to my sister. Apparently, my mother had amended her will; in the previous version, she had divided her estate equally between my sister and me. If I didn't contest the trust, I would get the money in 120 days. My mother had essentially disinherited me, which, of course, had been her right. In the document, it enumerated that if my sister, who was the primary beneficiary, and the secondary beneficiary, and the tertiary beneficiary were to predecease my mother, I would be considered to have predeceased her too.

Over my dead body, she seemed to be saying.

A long time ago, in a city nicknamed Berzerkeley, we, the cohort, were children. Our parents were professors and mail carriers, architects and bus drivers, civil servants and housewives. We were of different races, classes, and ethnicities; raised Christian, Jewish, Buddhist, Muslim, or to be nonbelievers; the daughters and sons of people who, by chance or choice, happened to be living in the Bay Area in the 1960s. We were at ground zero of the Free Speech Movement as the Civil Rights Movement and the Feminist Movement spread across the land. We were the kids prophesied in *Free to Be...You and Me*, a 1972 album produced by Marlo Thomas and the Ms. Foundation for Women that promotes gender equality, tolerance, and the radical notion that anyone can achieve anything, the title track of which foreshadows a land in which the children are free.

When we were around ten, there was a reunion at the Blocks' house in Kensington, not far from the pink stucco house in which my parents' marriage was silently imploding. I recall being there, a lot of children milling around, and lingering on the periphery because I was shy (still am, honestly). For that one day, I had been in the same room with the rest of the cohort, or most of them (some of the others had moved away by then, although many of them would continue to be tracked by the study for years). Somewhere in my brain, they were still there, having made an impression that over the years had become a faded imprint.

In fact, a few were there all along. There was 183, whom I had known, the boy who had been in my grade school classroom, whose parents had known my parents, and who would reveal to me when I called him that he had been in the study, but he had dropped out around the time he had reached adolescence because his parents' marriage was not in good shape, and the idea of sharing that with strangers (the researchers) had been mortifying to him. There was 429, one of those nerdy girls whom I had befriended in the eighth grade, and who related to me that her mother had removed her from the study in preschool because her mother didn't like the idea of researchers studying her daughter: Who knew what kind of effect it would have on a little girl? And there was 566, a girl who was athletic, and sweet, and tall, and whom I had been friendly with in high school, and who had, I learned, had died, tragically, in her thirties.

And then there was the day in Berkeley, when I was sitting at my desk at the IRP, and an email with a strange subject header appeared in my inbox. *Fellow human lab rat?* it read. The email was from a man who lived in the Bay Area and was a few years older than me. He had seen a thumbnail photo of me in a marketing email from a dating site of which I had been but was no longer a member. Intrigued, he had used that image to figure out who I was by searching the internet. When he had read about the research I was doing at the IRP, he had realized there was a curious coincidence. He had attended a similar preschool run by UC Berkeley around the corner from the Child Study Center, and his late brother had attended the same preschool I had and had been a member of the Block Project cohort, too. Online I searched the name of the man who had sent me the email. He was handsome, successful, taller than me. We agreed to meet for coffee. In the time between when

I received his email and our date, I wondered if my story might lead me to someplace I hadn't expected: to love. He was nice, smart, and kind, and I was interested, but while he sent me a few emails after that, he didn't ask me out again.

So it goes, I thought.

———

The twisted roots of longitudinal studies are entangled in eugenics and buried in Silicon Valley. In 1921, Lewis Terman, a Stanford psychologist and prominent eugenicist who believed intelligence was inherited and advocated the forced sterilization of the "feebleminded," commenced Genetic Studies of Genius, the oldest and longest-running longitudinal study. At that time, gifted children were viewed as "pathetic creatures, overserious and undersized, hollow-chested, stoop-shouldered, clumsy, tense, and neurotic," who, as adults, went insane, drifted into obscurity, or otherwise failed to live up to their early promise. Terman, who had been a gifted child himself, set out to prove "genius" children were stronger, taller, and healthier than their less gifted peers and were biologically destined for greatness. Using his version of an intelligence test created by Alfred Binet and Théodore Simon, the Binet-Simon test—a revised version of Terman's test, the Stanford-Binet Intelligence Scales, is one of the most widely used intelligence tests today—he curated a cohort of over a thousand schoolchildren with IQ scores of 135 or higher from across California (problematically, their number included his own son and daughter) and studied them for decades. But Terman was unable to resist meddling in his subjects' lives. Behind the scenes, he pulled strings that got "my gifted children," as he always referred to his subjects, into the best colleges and out of legal troubles. Ultimately, while some "Termites," as they were known, went on to lead remarkable lives, many didn't, and Terman was forced to concede: "At any rate, we have seen that intellect and achievement are far from perfectly correlated." (According to "The Vexing Legacy of Lewis Terman," which appeared in the July/August 2000 issue of *Stanford Magazine*, "two children who were tested but *didn't* make the cut—William Shockley and Luis Alvarez—went on to win the Nobel Prize in Physics. [...But] none of the Terman kids ever won a Nobel or Pulitzer.") IQ *wasn't* destiny.

Regardless, being studied had proved life altering for many of Terman's subjects. A quarter of the male subjects and nearly a third of the female subjects reported that being a "Terman kid" had changed their lives. For some, the "genius" label had given them the confidence to reach heights they might not have otherwise. For others, the moniker had been a burden under which they'd floundered, struggling to live up to the expectations of being labeled gifted. Still others would never know if or to what degree Terman's puppeteering had shaped their trajectories.

As I neared writing the ending of my book, I weighed the impact of being studied on my life. As a retired UC Berkeley psychology professor who had conducted longitudinal intervention studies that sought not to merely observe but to intercede in their subjects' lives and who described our dataset as "tremendous and beautiful" had told me of our cohort: "Everyone who was in the study would be affected by the study." Were it not for the Block Project, I would not have embarked on my investigative journey. In doing so, I became my own observer effect, changing the story of my life as I revisited, revised, and retold it. Essentially, the adult me was the one my younger self sensed watching through the one-way mirror of a Tolman Hall experiment room. Being studied had changed my life, in more ways than one.

One afternoon eight months after my mother died, I took a break from writing and drove west on US Route 101. I exited at Woodman Avenue in Sherman Oaks and went to the Antique Mall. I had been thinking about the tin dollhouse I had as a girl; I wanted to buy one like it. In a back room, I spotted a row of dollhouses like the one I had. I bought a dollhouse that looked most like the one I remembered and a couple dozen pieces of the small plastic furniture that went with it. At home, I ordered a few of the figures that were made for the dollhouse from Etsy. A week later, the package arrived. I examined the people; their identities were stamped onto the bottom of their bases: MOTHER, FATHER, SISTER. I sat on the floor arranging the dolls and the furnishings in the dollhouse, ignoring the voice in my head telling me I was *too old* to play with a dollhouse. The mother, whose left hand was on her hip, stood in the kitchen, staring, as if she were annoyed, at a child, who was supposed to be me, sitting on the fake-linoleum floor. The sister went in an upstairs bedroom, looking out the window, as if she wanted to be elsewhere. The father, whose right hand grasped a pipe, held court in the living room, facing the part of the dollhouse that was open, as if he were about to deliver an important speech to an invisible audience.

The tumor baby would be around the same age I was when my parents broke up, I considered as I moved things around. It would have a different outcome than I had, I was certain. Its parents would not divorce. It would not have to spend a long time trying not to feel things it did not want to feel. It would be happy, flourishing, its authentic self.

On Mother's Day, I finished writing my book. I sat back and stared at the words. I didn't have a husband or children or a fairy tale ending, but I had the book I had long wanted to write. In writing it, I had become the author of the story of my life. I closed the document and opened my browser. A long time ago, personality researchers had spied on me. Now tech companies with multi-billion-dollar valuations were surveilling me. Every day, as I surfed the internet, used my phone, or drove my car, my data was being mined and monetized—and it was all done with my consent. In our brave new tech world, Big Brother is watching us, and the goal isn't scientific enlightenment but social engineering for profit. These days, we're all data babies. Somewhere a little girl is being co-parented by a digital device, and it isn't seeking to predict her future but to tell her who she is and what she wants, steer her behavior and decide for her.

Who will *she* grow up to be?

ACKNOWLEDGMENTS

A special thanks to: Lydia Netzer, for telling me to nut up and write; Sarah Catania, for being in the memoir trenches with me; Vickie Pynchon, for sharing her wisdom; Mina Merkel, for the sage advice; Geryll Robinson, for being my guide; Justin Cohen, Matt Young, and Camas Davis, for the camaraderie; Peternelle van Arsdale, for being my editor; Mollie Glick, for being my agent; and Creative Artists Agency, for the rest; Hachette Book Group, for publishing this book; Tim Weiner, for picking me; Sarah Stillman, for encouraging me; Thread at Yale, for the storytelling space; the Logan Nonfiction Program, for the magic room; UC Berkeley's Investigative Reporting Program, for the fellowship; Geeta Anand, for listening; the Minions— Betty Márquez Rosales, Casey Smith, Cecilia Lei, and Ali DeFazio—for helping me; the International Women's Media Foundation's Howard G. Buffett Fund for Women Journalists, for the support; the Social Science Summer Institute for Journalists at the Russell Sage Foundation,

ACKNOWLEDGMENTS

for the seminar; the Block Project, for selecting me for the cohort; my mother, for enrolling me in the preschool; my father, for showing me what a person who writes books looks like and inspiring me to do the same; and my therapist, Michael Bader, for making me feel less crazy and never giving up on me.